The World's Great
Adventure Treks

GENERAL EDITOR: JACK JACKSON

Abbeville Press   New York   London

THE WORLD'S GREAT
ADVENTURE TREKS

First published in the United States of America in 2005 by Abbeville Press

First published in Great Britain in 2003 by New Holland Publishers

Book design and layout copyright © 2003 New Holland Publishers (UK) Ltd
Text copyright © 2003 individual authors as listed on pages 152-153
Maps copyright © 2003 New Holland Publishers (UK) Ltd
Photographs © 2003 individual photographers and/or their agents as
listed on page 157

Library of Congress Cataloging-in-Publication Data

The world's great adventure treks / general editor, Jack Jackson.
   p. cm.
"First published in Great Britain in 2003 by New Holland Publishers"—T.p.verso.
Includes bibliographical references and index.
ISBN 0-7892-0847-4 (alk. paper)
1. Hiking—Guidebooks. 2. Adventure travel—Guidebooks. I. Jackson,
Jack, 1938-

GV199.5.W67 2005
796.52'2—dc22
         2004021125

PUBLISHER AND EDITOR Mariëlle Renssen
MANAGING EDITORS Claudia dos Santos, Simon Pooley
DESIGNER Peter Bosman
COMMISSIONING EDITOR Simon Pooley
CARTOGRAPHY Carl Germishuys
ILLUSTRATION Maryna Beukes, Steven Felmore
PICTURE RESEARCH Karla Kik
PRODUCTION Myrna Collins
GENERAL EDITOR Jack Jackson
PROOFREADER Katja Splettstoesser
INDEXER Leizel Brown

REPRODUCTION BY
Hirt & Carter (Cape) Pty Ltd
PRINTED AND BOUND IN SINGAPORE BY
Tien Wah Press (Pte) Ltd

2 4 6 8 10 9 7 5 3 1

HALF TITLE *Climbers traversing the Evans glacier, near the head of the Whitcombe River, in New Zealand's Southern Alps.*

FULL TITLE *Using ski poles to aid them through the thick snow, three heavily laden backpackers cross the Hevek River via a suspension bridge, in the Kaçkar, Turkey.*

ABOVE *Camping on Vista Pass in the Bridger Wilderness, located in the Wind River range of the Wyoming Rockies; this forms part of the Highline Trail.*

OVERLEAF *Making progress, step by step (pole, pole, as the locals advise), at a height of 4500m (14,800ft), heading to the Kibo crater on Mount Kilimanjaro, Tanzania.*

CONTENTS

ABOVE *In the high mountain-desert region of Ladakh, northern India, parts of the Zanskar River freeze every winter. Here, villagers use the ice as a means to gain access to other villages.*

GREENLAND

Baffin Bay

Alaska

Anchorage •
**Alaska on Foot
(p. 40)**

*Great Bear
Lake*

*Great
Slave Lake*

*Lake
Athabasca*

Hudson
Bay

CANADA

*Lake
Winnipeg*

**Continental
Divide (p. 46)** •

Montana

*Great
Lakes*

London •

**Sawtooth Traverse
(p. 34)**

Idaho

Woming

**Way
St Jam
(p. 10**

California

**Highline Trail
(p. 28)**

**Picos de Europa
(p. 106)** •

San Francisco •

**Evolution Loop
(p. 22)**

UNITED STATES
OF AMERICA

Washington DC •

Madrid •

SPAIN

Phoenix •

Gulf of
Mexico

CUBA

SAH

Caribbean
Sea

West Indies

PACIFIC OCEAN

SOUTH
AMERICA

PERU

Lima •

Inca Trail (p. 60)

N

CHILE

ATLANTIC OCEA

Santiago •

MAP KEY

Treks covered by this book •

Capital city or major city •

**Exploradores
Valley (p. 54)** •

2000   4000 miles

2000   4000   6000 kilometres

ASIA

EUROPE

Stockholm

Lake
Baikal

**Kharkhiraa &
Turgen (p. 92)**

Ulaanbaatar

MONGOLIA

GREECE

Black Sea

Ankara

Caspian
Sea

Aral
Sea

Lake
Balkhash

North Pindos
Mountains
(p. 112)

Athens

TURKEY

**Kaçkar of the
Pontic Alps
(p. 68)**

Iraklíon

CRETE

**Across the Spine
of Crete (p. 118)**

**Lukpe La
(p. 74)**

Islamabad

**Zanskar River
(p. 80)**

CHINA

**Tiger's Lair & Sacred Peak
(p. 86)**

DESERT

Red Sea

PAKISTAN

New
Delhi

BHUTAN

PACIFIC OCEAN

INDIA

Hong Kong

AFRICA

PHILIPPINES

Lake
Victoria

SRI
LANKA

TANZANIA

**Mount Kilimanjaro
(p. 146)**

Lake
Tanganyika

Dodoma

INDONESIA

NEW GUINEA

INDIAN OCEAN

Timor Sea

Darwin

Hinchinbrook
Island

**Thorsborne Trail
(p. 126)**

Great Barrier Reef

AUSTRALIA

Johannesburg

SOUTH
AFRICA

**Northern Drakensberg
(p. 140)**

Durban

Perth

Sydney

Cape Town

NEW ZEALAND

Tasmania

Wellington

Tasman
Sea

**Āoraki to Arthur's
Pass (p. 132)**

INTRODUCTION

By JACK JACKSON

What is an adventure trek? Originally a trek referred to migration by ox-wagon but nowadays it can cover any form of transport on land. The Collins English Dictionary quotes 'a long and often difficult journey', particularly one that occurs in stages. With respect to trekking, 'adventure' is more difficult to define. The Collins English Dictionary gives 'a risky undertaking of unknown outcome' or 'an exciting or unexpected event or course of events'. Other dictionaries go further, quoting 'a hazardous activity'.

For this book we have concentrated on trekking on foot rather than by animals or vehicles, but the word adventure means different things to different people. Essentially, an adventure is something that an individual chooses to do, and any risk involved is self-imposed – so the individual decides what level of adventure or risk he or she is willing to accept. Trekkers with little experience of mountains will find the Inca Trail in Peru or hiking across Crete just as adventurous as trekking in high mountains; and those keen on religion will find designated religious pilgrimages just as fulfilling.

When establishing the criteria for treks in this book, with the exception of the Way of St James, we decided on the following:

1 The trek must be in a region that is not routinely traversed except by the local people.
2 The trek requires careful planning and/or expert guidance.
3 The region trekked through has very little infrastructure.
4 The trek passes through remarkable terrain.
5 It is at least five days' duration of active trekking from the point of departure to the end of the trek (not from arrival in the country or region).

6 The distance covered is at least 96km (60 miles), although to some extent this depends on the difficulty of the terrain crossed and how much ascent and descent is involved.
7 It is challenging in terms of fitness and/or psychological stamina.
8 The trek should not involve anything too technical, i.e. no advanced specialist skills are required (at least, not by most of the trekkers on organized treks).
9 The trek should involve an element of risk, or (at least potential) exposure to danger, the unknown or the unexpected.

Items 1 and 9 may require further explanation. With physical fitness, one tends to overexert on day one, ache like hell on day two, feel better on day three, then feel comfortably fit for the rest of the trek. On commercial treks, the first day is usually arranged so that if any of the participants demonstrate really poor physical fitness, they can still be easily returned to the point of departure and, if necessary, repatriated. Psychologically, things are the reverse: some people are affected in weird ways by altitude, others do not sleep well at night and after a week of bad nights do inept things such as being constantly unpleasant to other group members, or falling over and breaking bones. A common problem is for people who are on a regular prescription medication to forget to take it. This often has disastrous results for the rest of the party.

In terms of the risk element, the enjoyment of a trek often involves taking on a genuinely challenging journey; trekking along a slippery mountain trail where one side has a large drop into a river; trekking along a narrow ridge in a high wind; or wading across rivers.

ABOVE *A trekker pauses to chat to two locals in the Çaymakur valley, part of the Kaçkar mountain-trek in the Anatolian range of northeastern Turkey.*

ABOVE *Pausing on the contour path beneath Giant's Castle, hikers are dwarfed by the immensity of the Drakensberg massif, KwaZulu-Natal, South Africa.*

Basic trekking can be enjoyed with the minimum of equipment so long as one can read a map and use a compass. However, the introduction of satellites, hi-tech equipment and clothing has made a huge difference in the last 40 years. In the 1960s many countries forbade the issue of accurate maps for civilian use. The best that I could find for trekking in Afghanistan and the Sahara Desert were British Military Survey Tactical Pilotage Charts, the aviation charts used by aircraft pilots – hardly a large enough scale for accurate route-finding on foot! Communications then were rudimentary, some military posts had field telephones, though few of these worked.

By the early 1970s, many remote settlements had satellite communication powered by diesel generators. Using one of these was like using a ship's radio; you spoke, waited a few seconds, heard an echo of your own voice and then received a reply. Nowadays, there are still a few places where communication remains a problem, but for those who can afford them, there are portable satellite telephones and video transmission systems for remote use, even on the summit of Everest. More useful are Global Positioning System receivers. Now that the degraded civilian signal has been discontinued, so long as there is not heavy tree or mountain cover between the receiver and the satellites, we can all receive the military-quality signal, which gives us a position accurate to a few metres horizontally. However, electronics and batteries regularly fail, so carry at least two receivers and several spare batteries.

Large-scale maps are now available for most trekking areas and new technology has given us lightweight clothing, and lighter trekking boots, tents and cooking equipment. Backpacks are better designed for carrying loads, and trekking poles help reduce stress on the knees and lower back when walking downhill, while dehydrated food is more scientifically designed.

ABOVE *Single-file on a path high above the Paro Chuu River in northern Bhutan; the highlight of this trek is the giant Himalayan ice peak, Chomolhari.*

New technology has done more than make existing treks easier. It has enabled us to take on longer and more adventurous routes, and improvements in transportation mean that we can trek in remoter regions.

Treks need not be a wilderness experience; there may be continuous habitation though individual houses and settlements may be quite far apart. Trekkers may have to arrange air or boat transport to the point where they commence their trek, and a pick-up from the point where they intend to finish. Treks are also not climbing trips – there may be places where some scrambling is necessary or the wearing of crampons is advisable, but no technical rock or ice-climbing should be required.

ABOVE *Hikers sidle around St Winifred's stream in the Havelock valley in New Zealand's Southern Alps; this valley in particular has an abundance of huts, which is reassuring to parties encountering storms and bad weather.*

BACKPACKING TREKS

In populated areas, backpackers can rely on local overnight accommodation, so they do not have to carry tents, cooking equipment and food. Depending on the region that they are trekking in, local meals can get very repetitive and if there are many trekkers around, hostelries and teahouses can be temporarily out of food, so for both reasons some tasty high-energy, high-carbohydrate snacks should be carried. In some areas, participants in this type of trekking are at high risk of catching diseases spread by contaminated food, drink and poor hygiene, so they should be well versed in the various possible symptoms and carry the appropriate medications to treat such diseases.

SELF-CONTAINED TREKS

There are many remote regions where self-contained trekking is either necessary or especially enjoyable and there are others where it is unnecessary but it saves money. There is a limit to the amount of weight that anyone can carry comfortably day after day and still be able to enjoy the trek, but one has to carry the basic necessities of tent, sleeping bag and mat, clothing, cooking equipment, fuel, food, and items for water purification and personal hygiene. In general this means buying the lightest and most expensive equipment and food available. Living on freeze-dried or dehydrated food for more than two weeks at a time can drain your energy, so it is best to pack some high-carbohydrate foods as well. In some areas, fuel- and food-dumps can be set up but nowadays there are fewer and fewer countries where the contents are not likely to be stolen.

On this type of trekking, participants have the least chance of catching diseases spread by contaminated food, drink and poor hygiene, but in remote areas it is preferable that at least one member of the party has some medical training and carries a good medical kit.

DO-IT-YOURSELF TREKS

Given the time, it is possible to gather permits, porters or pack-animals, cooks, food and equipment, and set out with the same comforts and facilities as those of a trek arranged through a local trekking agency and travel agent in your country of residence. The advantage of porters is that they can carry the possessions that you do not require during the day so your personal trekking is made more enjoyable by not having to carry the weight. As well as carrying larger, more comfortable tents, they will also be able to carry stools or folding chairs and a much more varied selection of food. A properly organized trek will also have porters carrying kerosene or liquid petroleum gas for cooking so that local trees are not cut for firewood, and some porters will be designated to dig latrines. This method of trekking is particularly enjoyable for a group of friends.

On the downside you may have to send out someone in advance to fully complete the arrangements, there may be a problem with language and keeping control of porters, you have no way of knowing the honesty of those that you hire, and they may well charge you more than the going rate. Porters hired in this

way routinely strike for more pay after the first few days. In some countries it may be law that treks have to be organized through a registered trekking company in order to obtain a trekking permit. But so long as it is legal, if you work with people recommended by friends, you are likely to have an enjoyable trek.

With this type of trekking, participants have a good chance of catching diseases spread by contaminated food, drink and poor hygiene. At least one member of your party should have some medical training, carry a good medical kit and watch over the cook's hygiene when preparing food.

COMMERCIAL TREKS

In this instance, complete arrangements are made through a local trekking agency and a travel agent in your country of residence. This will be the most expensive option but it saves a lot of time and frustration. Participants will not have communication problems or trouble getting permits. The porters and cooks will be tried, tested and of proven honesty, fuel for cooking will be carried so that local trees are not cut for firewood and some porters will be organized to dig latrines. There will be a designated local leader who speaks the group's language and acts as a go-between/translator between the group and the porters, cooks and local people; and the cooks will have been trained in the necessary hygiene when preparing food. Money hassles are almost eliminated, the local leader is responsible for any minor purchases required along the way, and he can help the individual members of the party with personal bargaining. Many commercial trekking companies offer reduced rates to qualified doctors who are willing to act as official doctors while on a trek.

Two major advantages of a commercial trek come about because the local agent will have contacts all along the route. In any emergency, either back at home or on the trek, messages can be passed along the route in either direction. In countries that are no longer 100 per cent safe, a large party is organized, and the porters have an intimate knowledge of the area and the local people. This means that the party is less likely to attract trouble. In fact, in

ABOVE *The remoteness of many adventure trek regions makes self-sufficiency vital;
all food, cooking and personal hygiene requirements need to be carried in and out.*

ABOVE *Local guides who accompany trekking parties into the Himalaya in northern Bhutan are also made responsible for the cooking of all meals.*

some countries, the agency will have already paid off the local trouble-makers so that their trekker clients are left well alone.

In some countries, local law will insist that the trek is actually led by a local national, while in some of the trekkers' countries of residence, for reasons of litigation, a person who has passed, say, a two-week course and gained some form of mountain leadership certificate will be given precedence as agency group-leader over someone with 30 years of Himalayan experience. It is quite common for the porters to be very poorly paid and therefore heavily reliant on gratuities from the group as acceptable remuneration for their work – so cost in a decent tip.

PHYSICAL QUALIFICATIONS

By their very nature, treks are physically demanding. Commercial trekking brochures contain 'brochure-speak' that can fall anywhere between making relatively easy trips sound like major expeditions and quite difficult treks sound easy – most commercial treks are not that difficult. Older people who have completed many treks over many years are usually very good at doggedly placing one foot in front of the other when they feel tired. Treks organized for photographers to have plenty of time to take photographs can only cover short distances each day. Such treks are ideal for older people. The greatest deterrent is a history of knee or hip problems. Diabetics should carry the correct medicaments and sweet foods, and consume them regularly; this is particularly important at altitude. Note: It is important that the Western group leader or doctor is informed of any diabetic so that suitable action can be taken if necessary.

PERSONAL SAFETY

Several of the areas where groups have trekked safely in the past are now subject to civilian or religious strife, and other events are likely to occur in the future. It is important to keep up to date on the advice given by your government's Foreign Office Travel Advice unit.

PASSPORTS AND PERMITS

Before requesting visas – or if these are not necessary, before departure – your passport should be valid for six months longer than the expected length of the trip and have six empty pages left to cover any bureaucracy. Some countries will also require proof that you have suitable funds available and a return or onward air ticket. Some countries even require onward air tickets for overland travellers and others require a letter of introduction from your own government.

Never have photographer, writer, journalist or member of the armed forces mentioned in your passport, unless you are travelling officially as such; these professions often require special visas. Carry spare passport photographs and several photocopies of all paperwork, and keep them separate from the originals. If an official wants to take any paperwork away, give him/her a photocopy, as this is often misplaced.

INSURANCE

Take out individual personal and medical insurance, preferably a scheme that flies you home by Air Ambulance in a serious emergency.

VACCINATIONS AND PROPHYLACTICS

Make sure that you have all the required vaccinations and that they will remain in date for the whole trip. The vaccine against cholera was proven to be useless and has not existed for over a decade but several books, articles and brochures still mention it. Some countries continue to ask for it, in which case you can obtain a certificate of exemption. Where treks pass through areas in which dangerous diseases such as malaria are common, it is essential to take the correct precautions and prophylactics.

ALTITUDE AND ACCLIMATIZATION

It is essential to acclimatize slowly to altitude. Serious mountain sickness usually occurs above 3650m (12,000ft) but it can occur as low as 2150m

ABOVE *This climb out of Megas Lakkos gorge, in the Greek Pindos mountains, reinforces the need for good physical fitness when venturing into wilderness areas.*

ABOVE *Water, more than anything else, is crucial to our survival, and trek stops such as this one on Tanzania's Mount Kilimanjaro are to be taken seriously.*

(7000ft). The old adage of 'going high' during the day but 'sleeping low' at night still applies. Most people have real problems if they are transported high by road or air instead of walking up over several days. People suffering from altitude sickness should be taken down to a much lower altitude as soon as possible. Drugs such as Acetazolamide (Diamox) can relieve the symptoms of benign mountain sickness – and can be used by those going to altitude only for a very short time – but these are no substitute for correct acclimatization.

FOOD AND WATER
Food that is cooked properly from the raw state should be safe to eat, but when cooked food, such as rice and meat, is allowed to cool, some of the organisms that grow on these foods are not killed by reheating. This can be a problem in the type of higher-quality hotel that trekkers often use before and after a trek. Many hotels reheat precooked food or leave food standing around as a buffet for many hours where flies or cockroaches can contaminate it.

When purchasing bottled water in the Third World, make sure that the seal is intact and do not contaminate the water by adding ice. The only way to be sure of purifying local water is to boil it vigorously for at least 20 minutes, longer at altitude. If you are above the snow line, you will save work and fuel by melting ice rather than snow. Chlorine tablets will not kill amoeba in the cyst form; this requires iodine, which some people are allergic to. Iodine tablets or a small dropper bottle containing tincture of iodine can be used to quickly purify the water supplied in cheap restaurants. Unless they are combined with chemical treatment, the filters sold in camping shops will not filter out tiny organisms such as viruses. They will also block up quickly if the water contains fine grit from glacier meltwater.

ABOVE *Neglecting to acclimatize in high altitudes leads to nasty headaches, and worse, can bring on altitude sickness, which must be dealt with immediately.*

RAMADAN

The Muslim fasting month of Ramadan should be avoided in Islamic countries. In 1977 I had a week to get from a trek that I had led in Ladakh, India, to a trek starting in Gilgit, Pakistan. In the days of the British Raj I could have walked across from Srinagar in a matter of days, but with the problems between India and Pakistan, my flights via Delhi and Lahore were held up; I arrived a day late. The group that I was to lead had arrived the day before – the last day of Ramadan. During this holy month, Muslims must not consume food or drink during the day, so, in my absence, when the group had a hotel lunch, the food had been reheated from the day before. Reheated rice and meat is highly questionable. Within a few days, most of them were sick and they got worse throughout the trek. Most members of the group were doctors and they became more and more convinced that they had typhoid. However, on their return to the UK, tests proved the problem to be giardiasis (*Giardia lamblia*), which could have been easily treated during the trek.

ACCIDENTS

In 1974, while on what was then a remote trek among hill tribes on the northern Thailand–Burma (now Myanmar) border, my group one night were dancing with the family in the yard of the dwelling where we were staying. One lady tripped over and broke her leg. We were four days' walk from the nearest river and then a further half-day from the nearest hospital – so my main concern was not the break but infection.

Transporting her back to safety was a major undertaking. We constructed a bamboo stretcher and gathered local porters to carry it – but it was not that simple. Many of the villages were at war with each other, so I had to keep finding fresh porters since each group would only carry her as far as the next village. Then at each village, the inhabitants were superstitious about carrying an injured person through their settlement, and I had to buy a chicken to be sacrificed before we could continue. I am not a doctor, though I do have some expedition medical training, so I risked giving her broad-spectrum antibiotics for the time it took to reach an American mission hospital in Chiang Mai. Fortunately we saved her leg and she was able to do another trip with me later. Even the best organized of treks can have problems – but they are rare.

PERSONAL ENJOYMENT OF A TREK

There are many reasons to enjoy trekking, not least because it is a physical activity. Some people take pleasure from captivating natural scenery and, where they exist, the exotic and diverse cultures of local ethnic groups living a subsistence lifestyle. Others prefer harsh environments and extreme terrain, while those on a pilgrimage have the satisfaction of making the journey for religious, respectful, nostalgic or sentimental reasons. Photographers do not have to dash to the next viewpoint but are able to stop and photograph often, allowing for different views and the nuances of the light. Spectacular views, including the sight of early morning cloud rising from the valley floor like steam from a boiling kettle in Himalayan high mountains, embed themselves in one's memory. When well clear of light pollution in the wilds, the bright stars in a clear sky at night are amazing. In 1971, while bivouacking in the Sahara Desert, a shower of shooting stars appeared to be so close that we felt they might hit us. Finding oneself incredibly close to wild animals can be rewarding, too. We came across bears near Skardu in Pakistan, lynx in Morocco, desert foxes in the Sahara, bearded vultures (lammergeiers) in Afghanistan and Pakistan, griffon vultures in Yemen, ptarmigan in Iceland, and wolves attacking sheep in Iran. Travelling with local porters, interacting with the local people and residing with them overnight can be very satisfying, especially when the trek coincides with local festivals. My treks have involved: being guests of honour at a polo final and the presentation of the winners' cup in Gilgit, and at a fantasia in Morocco; having tea with the Mir of Hunza when it was still an autonomous state, dinner with the Mir of Punial in Pakistan and the Gurkha chief of staff in Ladakh; breaking Ramadan fasts with Afghan and Iranian chiefs and a Pakistani general; having coffee with an Iranian princess, joining several marriage feasts in Yemen and regularly being certified as alcoholics to legally obtain supplies of beer in Pakistan since it went dry!

All in all, why laze on the beach for a vacation when you can opt for an adrenaline-inducing adventure and see the world in a different way? If you take pleasure from walking, then this book and the regions featured within it will provide inspiration for that next enterprise. Enjoy your trekking!

OPPOSITE *Truly awe-inspiring natural scenery, such as this in the central Sahara, Algeria, is one of the most gratifying aspects of travelling to remote destinations.*

ABOVE *There are those who settle on harsh, unforgiving terrain as their idea of adventure; this does, however, demand a high level of careful planning.*

EVOLUTION LOOP

Sky gardens of the High Sierra

Sierra Nevada, California, USA

RALPH STORER

The incomparable Sierra Nevada (Spanish for 'snowy mountains') is one of the world's most beautiful and hikeable mountain ranges. It is formed of the largest continuous block of granite in the world, measuring 675km (420 miles) long and 95–125km (60–80 miles) wide. The block is tilted to the west such that the imposing eastern front towers 3050m (10,000ft) and more over the Owens valley to form one of the great escarpments of the world. On the west the mountains fade away into forested rolling hills, but there is also some surprisingly spectacular scenery here, where ice has carved dramatic canyons, such as Yosemite, deep into the high country.

The central part of the range, known as the High Sierra, is a hikers' paradise uncrossed by road for 250km (160 miles). Finely sculptured mountains, 500 of them higher than 3650m (12,000ft) and 11 'Fourteeners' (mountains over 14,000ft, or 4270m) pierce the blue sky above enchanting lakes and beautiful alpine meadows and basins. Monarch of the range is Mount Whitney, at 4420m (14,495ft) the highest mountain in the USA outside of Alaska, a magnificent peak with a trail all the way to its summit.

As if the scenery were not enough, the Sierra has the mildest, sunniest climate of any of the world's major mountain ranges. Only five per cent of the annual average precipitation falls between the beginning of July and the end of September, with an occasional afternoon thunderstorm. Average summer midday temperature at 3050m (10,000ft) is 16°C (60°F).

The range encompasses three national parks, 17 wildernesses and eight national forests. Yosemite and Kings Canyon national parks are centred on the

two most spectacular canyons, while Sequoia National Park celebrates the giant sequoia trees for which the snowy range is famous. Outside the parks there is equally beautiful country that gives incomparable high-elevation hiking opportunities far from the crowds.

The classic High Sierra trek is the John Muir Trail (JMT), which runs for 336km (210 miles) along the length of the range, from the summit of Mount Whitney in the south to Yosemite in the north. John Muir was a Scottish immigrant whose love of these mountains made him America's pioneer conservationist. It was through his efforts that Yosemite became established as a national park in 1890.

The JMT offers an unforgettable rollercoaster hike across numerous high passes through memorable scenery. The complete trip is a major undertaking requiring a minimum of three weeks and at least one break to walk or hitchhike to the nearest town for new supplies. Owing to time constraints, most vacationing backpackers will be content to sample the trail, and there is no finer introduction than the Evolution Loop.

This magnificent circular trip begins at a high trailhead on the east side of the Sierra crest and loops over high passes to the west side to explore some of the loveliest terrain in the range. The beautiful meadows found above the

OPPOSITE INSET *The craggy slopes of Mount Spencer, towering above Evolution Lake, glow red-hot in the sunset light.*

OPPOSITE *The trail enters Dusy basin on the west side of Bishop Pass. The prominent peak on the left is Columbine, attained by a scramble on the far side.*

TOP *Trekkers descend into the basin on the South Lake side of Bishop Pass. Bishop Lake (left) and Ledger Lake (right) are only two of many lakes here.*

ABOVE RIGHT *A desolate but beautiful campsite beside the ice flows of Wanda Lake at the head of Evolution basin, with the craggy skyline of Mount Goddard.*

PREVIOUS PAGES *A bright tangle of wildflowers – arrowleaf balsamroot and lupins – captured on film in the Bitterroot mountains.*

LOCATION High Sierra Nevada mountains, central California, USA.

WHEN TO GO July to October, with snow on high passes until early August, and sometimes all summer at Muir Pass.

START South Lake trailhead (2975m; 9755ft), 34km (21 miles) southwest along Highway 168 from Bishop, on US 395.

FINISH North Lake trailhead (2870m; 9415ft), 32km (20 miles) southwest along Highway 168 from Bishop. Enquire locally about shuttle services between trailheads.

DURATION Minimum 8–10 days (84km; 52 miles).

MAX. ALTITUDE Muir Pass (3640m; 11,955ft).

TECHNICAL CONSIDER-ATIONS Trails are excellent throughout, but a trek of this length, remoteness and altitude should only be attempted by experienced backpackers. Several river fords are required. Camping necessary throughout.

EQUIPMENT Good boots, warm clothes and wet-weather gear, backpack, tent and sleeping gear, food and cooking utensils. Sunscreen and mosquito repellent.

TREKKING STYLE Backpacking, mostly above the timber line in spectacular high-altitude alpine country. Once onto the west side of the Sierra crest the country is remote, with no short escape routes. Backpacking at over 3050m (10,000ft) requires fitness and determination. You will acclimatize as you go, but plan for short days and allow time for rest days. In an emergency there are back-country ranger stations, manned in summer, in Le Conte canyon and Evolution valley.

PERMITS/RESTRICTIONS Permits are required for overnight back-country travel and should be booked well in advance from address below.

DANGERS Black bears are numerous in the High Sierra, especially in popular areas where they are used to humans. At forest campsites especially, cook and store food away from the tent. Streams may contain giardia. All drinking water should be boiled, filtered or treated with iodine.

MAPS USGS (United States Geological Survey) 1:63,360, John Muir Wilderness, National Parks Back-country. One map covers the central section of the JMT, the other covers the north and south sections. Both are required.

INFORMATION

Back-country Office, White Mountain Ranger District, 798 N. Main Street, Bishop, CA 93514; tel: +1-619-8734207.

Websites: www.bishopvisitor.com
www.r5.fs.fed.us/inyo

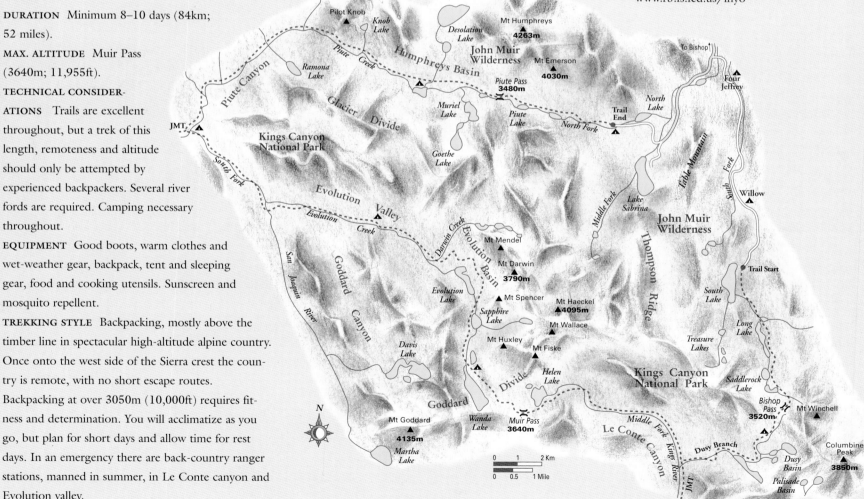

timber line provide idyllic camping in breathtaking high-country basins. John Muir called these high meadows 'sky gardens'. The highlight of the trek is Evolution basin in a remote part of the High Sierra between Kings Canyon and Yosemite, where the scenery is at least the equal of the two flanking national parks. The basin is so named because the peaks surrounding it are named after pioneer advocates of evolution: Darwin, Mendel, Huxley, Spencer, Haeckel, Wallace and Fiske.

The route begins at South Lake trailhead, 2975m (9755ft) above Bishop, and climbs about 10km (6 miles) past numerous lakes to Bishop Pass (3520m; 11,550ft). Unless you have already become acclimatized to the altitude, you may well wish to make a first camp beside one of these lakes. At the pass, the trail crosses the Sierra crest from east to west and enters the great, wide-open

ABOVE *Seen from Columbine Peak, the 4270m (14,000ft) Palisades tower over one of the Barrett Lakes in the Palisade basin.*
OPPOSITE *On the descent from Dusy basin into Le Conte canyon, the trail is accompanied by this giant waterslide.*

Dusy basin, where strings of lakes lie at the foot of Mount Winchell. It is worth taking a day out here to hike across the basin to Knapsack Pass and scramble up Columbine Peak (3850m; 12,652ft) for stunning views across neighbouring Palisade basin to the towering Palisades, the Sierra's most alpine mountains and home of its largest glaciers.

From Dusy basin the trail makes a long switchback descent beside the tumbling Dusy Branch into Le Conte canyon to meet the JMT at a back-country ranger station. On the way down you pass picturesque lakes, waterfalls and a huge waterslide that flows over granite slabs for hundreds of feet. Once on the JMT, height is regained on a long ascent that climbs Le Conte canyon to cross the Goddard Divide at Muir Pass (3640m; 11,955ft), the trek's highpoint. The length of this climb, the numerous stream crossings and tiring snow patches that may linger near the summit all summer may well prompt you into an overnight camp before tackling the final stretch.

Helen Lake on the near side of the pass and Wanda Lake on the far side are named after John Muir's daughters and make wonderfully desolate, if chilly, campsites. Early in the season, ice floes can be seen on each and on the even higher Lake McDermand just over the pass. Wanda Lake, especially, is gloriously colourful at sunset and dawn. At the summit of the pass is Muir Hut, a stone cabin erected as a memorial to the man himself. This provides shelter in foul weather or an emergency, but makes a less attractive overnight base than a lakeside camp. Note that from the pass to beyond Evolution Lake wood fires are prohibited.

Wanda Lake (3490m; 11,452ft) heralds the start of Evolution basin. The land is ice-scoured and naked, and feels even higher and more remote than it is. At the lake's outflow, the trail fords Evolution Creek and enters the stunning lower basin, whose flanking rock peaks tower overhead as you stroll from lake to lake. First come the impressive rock faces of arrow-like mounts Huxley and Fiske, then pointed Mount Spencer above Sapphire Lake, followed by the 910m (3000ft) wall of Mounts Mendel and Darwin above Evolution Lake.

Every new corner affords yet another flawless composition to be photographed. The far end of Evolution Lake at the foot of the basin has a few pine trees to soften the landscape and may well be the best campsite. When viewed from here at sunset, the 3790m (12,440ft) pyramid of Mount Spencer can look as if it were on fire. Its summit is a wonderful perch from which to view the surrounding country, and it is worth taking a day out to make the easy scramble up the granite slabs of the southeast ridge.

Below Evolution Lake the trail plunges in switchbacks into forested Evolution valley, which is followed down to its junction with Goddard canyon. The valley's beautiful but fragile meadows suffered from years of trampling before the decision was taken finally to reroute the trail around them to give the meadows a chance to recover. Another back-country ranger station is situated halfway along the valley.

The trail continues down Goddard canyon beside the South Fork of the San Joaquin River, which surges between high, narrow walls. Thankfully, all river crossings are bridged. The day's trek ends at the junction of Goddard canyon and Piute canyon, where there are lovely campsites hidden among tall pine trees beside the boiling river. This spot also marks the point where the JMT is left to complete the Evolution Loop by climbing Piute canyon and recrossing to the east side of the Sierra crest at Piute Pass.

The climb begins with an initial, steep ascent in Piute canyon, then levels off to a fork in Hutchison Meadow beneath Pilot Knob. The Piute Pass Trail goes right, fords French Creek and climbs out of the forest into Humphreys basin, a vast featureless bowl backed by monolithic Mount Humphreys. The trail stays high above the Trout Lakes, Muriel Lake and numerous others to reach Piute Pass (3480m; 11,423ft) just beyond Summit Lake.

The long ascent can be broken with a high camp in Humphreys basin, which gives one last night at altitude before crossing Piute Pass the following day. On the far side, the trail descends past Piute Lake and Loch Leven to re-enter civilization at North Lake trailhead. From here it is some 20km (12 miles) along the road to South Lake trailhead. Without using a shuttle service, you can get there by walking, hitchhiking or taking the trail 760m (2500ft) up and down across intervening Table Mountain. The latter option will require more determination than any you would have evinced so far!

ABOVE *The arrowhead peaks of Mount Spencer (left) and Mount Huxley (right) tower over Evolution Lake. Mount Spencer's summit perch is very scenic.*

OPPOSITE *Mount Haeckel (right) and the ridge left to Mount Darwin, seen across an icy unnamed lake from the summit of Mount Spencer.*

HIGHLINE TRAIL
Cresting the Winds

Wyoming Rockies, northwestern USA
RALPH STORER

If there is one mountain range that encapsulates the rugged beauty and wild grandeur of the Rocky mountains of northwest USA, it is Wyoming's Wind River range, known to its devotees simply as the Winds. Here, protected from development, is an area of nearly 405,000ha (one million acres) of designated wilderness, where you can walk among high mountains for days on end from one idyllic campsite to another through an incredibly complex landscape that reveals some new delight at every turn.

The Winds are uncrossed by paved road for 177km (110 miles) from south to north and 65km (40 miles) from east to west. Within this rough rectangle are to be found 23 'thirteeners' (mountains over 13,000ft, or 3960m), seven of the 10 largest glaciers in the USA outside of Alaska, over 110 cirques, 1300 lakes and 1285km (800 miles) of walking trails. This is truly spectacular mountain country, the peaks characterized by immense rock walls towering over achingly beautiful lakes. Seen from the west they form a stunning frieze of bare rock between yellow-green sagebrush and blue sky.

Two features make the Winds unique as a hiking destination. Firstly, the mountains were elevated in stages, with pause enough in-between for erosion to reduce their flanks to plains, which were then raised during the next stage of mountain building. The result is that the spine of the Winds, especially on the west, is separated from the Wyoming plains by a series of benches. The largest of these runs along the length of the range at a height of 3050m (10,000ft) and more. In places it is over 16km (10 miles) wide. This makes access to the heart of the range from high trailheads technically easy, but also causes hikers to underestimate altitude problems.

The second unique feature of the Wind River range is the series of ancient fault lines that run north to south beside the crest of the range, which here forms the Continental Divide. Many of the river and valley systems run along these faults, parallel to the crest rather than away from it, for many miles. The benches and valleys combine to provide the Winds trekker with an

opportunity that is unrivalled – to travel in high mountain terrain close to the spine of the range itself.

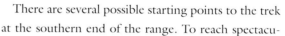 The ultimate Wind River backpacking trip combines the Highline Trail, which runs along the largest bench adjacent to the Divide, with detours to the Cirque of the Towers in the south of the range and Titcomb basin in the north. Omission of these two scenic highlights from the itinerary would be negligence bordering on criminal.

There are several possible starting points to the trek at the southern end of the range. To reach spectacular high country quickly, begin at Big Sandy trailhead and take the forest trail beside Big Sandy River to Big Sandy Lake (2950m; 9690ft). The 9km (6-mile) day makes an easy opener, while a two-night camp at the lake aids acclimatization and enables a packless day-hike to nearby Deep Lake. This lies in a craggy cirque backed by the sweeping mile-long rock wall of Haystack Peak and the rock spires of Steeple Peak, Lost Temple Spire and East Temple Peak. Adding to the ambience of the scene are the lakeside slabs that turn streams into a series of pools and waterslides. A return via Temple Lake completes a memorable day out.

From Big Sandy Lake it is a further 5km (3 miles) over Big Sandy Pass to Lonesome Lake at the heart of the Cirque of the Towers. The trail is surprisingly awkward and undulating, but the scenery more than compensates, with Sundance Pinnacle hovering over the ascent and the enormous face of Warbonnet almost overhanging the pass itself. Warbonnet is the first of the famed Towers that form a semicircle of rock peaks around Lonesome Lake. Others include the Warriors, Watch Tower, Sharks Nose, Overhanging Tower, Wolfs Head and, perhaps the most awesome of all, symmetrical Pingora Peak. After a night at Lonesome Lake, exit the cirque on the north side at Texas Pass

---

OPPOSITE INSET *The enormous truncated rock pillar of Squaretop Mountain, the symbol of the Winds, from the trail to Green River Lakes.*
OPPOSITE *Temple Lake and the trail from Temple Pass to Big Sandy Lake; a camp stop here on day one allows a day-hike to Deep Lake the following morning.*

TOP *As seen from the northwest ridge of Mount Lester above Little Seneca Lake, Titcomb basin reveals a dramatic, jagged skyline.*
ABOVE RIGHT *Crossing the granite slabs of Deep Lake Cirque with the Cirque of the Towers ahead; rising to the left is Warbonnet and to its right, Pingora.*

(3475m; 11,400ft), the trek's highpoint. More direct routes out of the cirque are difficult to negotiate and best avoided. The ascent to Texas Pass is easy, with any snow easily crossed, but the stone shoot on the far side carries only traces of a path and requires care. Lower down, a better trail descends past a series of lakes into the valley of Washakie Creek.

If a visit to the Cirque of the Towers seems too much at the beginning of the trip, you can avoid it altogether by following the Highline Trail marked on the map, which runs through forest west of the cirque. The Texas Pass route rejoins the Highline near Washakie Creek's confluence with the East Fork River, then heads northwestward across an open plateau below Mount Geikie. The plateau, at a height of 3200m (10,500ft), makes a scenic campsite with the southern part of the Winds spread out before you and the Towers glowing a ghostly white at sunset.

ABOVE *At the foot of the stone shoot on the north side of Texas Pass lies Texas Lake. The peak rising in the background is August 16th Peak.*

RIGHT *The remote peaks and pinnacles at the head of upper Titcomb basin provide mountaineering challenges of an almost expeditionary nature.*

Between the southern and northern parts of the range, a number of ridges jutting westwards from the Continental Divide give the hiker no option but to cross the middle part of the range below the timber line. There are many lakes, but as this section is the least scenic of the trip, it is best passed over in a long single day's trek. Of the many trails marked on the map, the shortest route follows the Old Highline and then the Fremont Trail.

The Fremont Trail emerges from the forest at Hat Pass (3306m; 10,848ft). A few more easy passes follow, then the scenery becomes breathtaking once again as you enter the northern part of the range at lake-studded Bald Mountain basin, with pointed Angel Peak to its right. A ford of Pole Creek, where you rejoin the Highline, and a crossing of Lester Pass bring you to Little Seneca Lake. This crossroads in the wilderness marks the spot where the Highline crosses the trail to Titcomb basin, and it is worth taking at least a day-hike detour if not a two- or three-day add-on backpack to visit this supreme example of Wind River mountain sculpture. If you do not have the time or energy, at least down your pack and climb onto the northwest ridge of Mount Lester for a view of Titcomb that will haunt you forevermore.

The side-trail to Titcomb goes over two low passes to Island Lake, whose islands, rocky headlands and sandy bays resemble an Aegean coastline. Behind the lake, Titcomb basin penetrates a further 10km (6 miles) into the highest peaks in the range, including Gannett – at 4207m (13,804ft) the tallest mountain in Wyoming. The best campsite is beside Pothole Lake, the first of the ribbon of lakes in the basin itself. From here you can spend one day exploring the lakes and the cirque of rock spires at the head of the basin, and another day exploring a side trail to beautiful Indian basin, whose heart is an amazing patchwork of rock and complex lake systems surrounded by 'thirteeners'.

Back at Little Seneca Lake, the Highline Trail makes a gradual ascent of the valley of Fremont Creek, passing lovely lakes, tumbling streams, snow patches and shapely rock spire. At Shannon Pass, which forms the head of the valley, the landscape becomes more intricately rocky and the trail threads a satisfying route down past rock bluffs and picturesque lakelets to emerge at Peak Lake Cirque. Much smaller than the Cirque of the Towers, the former has the air of a secret mountain sanctuary, with the giant arrowheads of Sulphur Peak (3909m; 12,825ft) and Stroud Peak (3718m; 12,198ft) seeming to hang overhead. Their sunset reflection in the lake is mesmerizing.

Peak Lake marks the end of high mountain country. North of here, the Highline crosses the easy Vista Pass before heading down into the Green River valley. It's a long walk out to Green River Lakes trailhead, but the pack is lighter now and there is still much to see. Most notable is Squaretop (3565m; 11,695ft), an enormous truncated rock pillar that has become the symbol of the range, because it is one of the few Wind River mountains that can be seen easily from points along the trail. You have become one of the privileged few who know that there are even more spectacular sights in the interior.

LEFT *The arrowhead of Stroud Peak hangs over a campsite in Peak Lake Cirque.*
OPPOSITE *In the foreground lies Island Lake, on the trail from Little Seneca Lake to Titcomb basin; the peak in the centre is Fremont, with Titcomb basin dipping to its left, and Indian basin to its right.*

LOCATION Wind River range (Rockies), northwest Wyoming, USA.

WHEN TO GO End July to mid-September. Expect snow in early season.

START Big Sandy trailhead, lodge and campground in the south (2775m; 9100ft), reached by dirt road from US 191 near Pinedale.

FINISH Green River Lakes trailhead and campground in the north (2430m; 7960ft), reached by dirt road from US 191 near Pinedale. Hitchhiking to and from trail-heads is normally easy, and a bus runs daily through Pinedale along US 191.

DURATION Minimum 8–10 days (103km; 64 miles).

MAX. ALTITUDE Texas Pass (3475m; 11,400ft).

TECHNICAL CONSIDERATIONS Trails are mostly good, but occasionally rough. Only experienced backpackers should attempt a trek of this length, remoteness and altitude. Snow may be encountered on the high passes at any time and may prove problematic in places until mid-August. Several river fords are required.

EQUIPMENT Good boots, warm clothes and wet-weather gear, backpack, tent, sleeping bag and mat, food and cooking utensils. Sunscreen and mosquito repellent are important.

TREKKING STYLE Backpacking, mostly above the timber line, in spectacular high-altitude alpine country. Camping is required throughout. Backpacking at over 3050m (10,000ft) requires fitness and determination; the Winds are remote mountains with no short escape routes. You will acclimatize as you go, but plan for short days and allow time for rest days.

PERMITS/RESTRICTIONS Apart from the Shoshone and Arapaho Wind River Indian Reservation on the east side of the Winds, the entire range has wilderness designation. Access to the trek described here is unrestricted. No permits are required.

DANGERS Black bears can be a problem at trailhead campsites and precautions should be taken everywhere, especially in forest; cook and store food away from tents. Streams may contain giardia. All drinking water should be boiled, filtered or treated with iodine.

MAPS *Northern Wind River range, Southern Wind River range*, 1:48,000 by Earthwalk Press.

INFORMATION

District Ranger, Pinedale Ranger District, PO Box 220, Pinedale, Wyoming 82941; tel: +1-307-3674326.

Websites: www.pinedaleonline.com; www.fs.fed.us/btnf

SAWTOOTH TRAVERSE
Secret cirques of the Sawtooths

Idaho Rockies, northwestern USA
RALPH STORER

The jagged Sawtooth mountains are part of the Rocky mountain system of the northwest USA. They are protected as the Sawtooth Wilderness, which is part of the 305,000ha (754,000-acre) Sawtooth National Recreation Area (SNRA). The SNRA was formed in 1972 as a conservation measure, in preference to a national park, in order to maintain the area's wilderness appeal.

The granite of which the Sawtooths are composed fractures easily, and this has enabled glaciation to carve them into fantastic splintered ridges and rock formations with evocative names like Fishhook Spire, Leaning Tower of Pisa, Finger of Fate and Arrowhead. The retreating glaciers have also left behind ice-scoured cirques filled by around 200 beautiful high-mountain lakes. Rarely has glaciation been more artistic.

In size 'the 'tooths', as they are known to those who love them, are about 50km (32 miles) long by 32km (20 miles) wide. They are large and complex enough to tempt backpackers into their rugged interior, but less overwhelming than other wilderness areas of northwest America. The spine of this range runs in a north–south line from McGown Peak (3000m; 9860ft) to Snowyside Peak (3245m; 10,651ft). Long, high side ridges branch off east and west, enclosing deep cirques and long valleys.

It is these side ridges that give the range a greater topographical complexity than would normally be expected in an area this size and make the range such a delight to explore. They contain some of the most interesting formations and the highest peak, Thompson Peak (3270m; 10,751ft). Altogether there are 33 peaks over 3050m (10,000ft).

While the western side of the range abuts the blanket forest that covers much of Idaho, the eastern side is more cleanly demarcated by the Sawtooth valley, a broad grassy depression that carries the great Salmon River, beloved of whitewater rafters. In an open basin at the north end of the valley lies the tiny settlement of Stanley, which has become the main base for exploration of the range and buzzes with activity during the summer season.

The eastern side is more popular than the western side. Eastern trailheads are higher and approaches to the high country shorter, with access roads from the Sawtooth valley leading to a series of large lakes around the 2100m (7000ft) mark. The eastern side also contains the greatest concentration of lakes and most compelling scenery. Many of the craggy summits are, not surprisingly, the preserve of rock climbers, so it is no wonder that they have become the home of Idaho mountaineering. But there are also sufficient easy passes between the peaks so that a 480km (300-mile) network of good trails could be laid out.

The classic Sawtooth trek is the north-to-south or south-to-north traverse of the range, an 82km (51-mile) trip that crosses five passes and stays on the east side of the main crest for most of its length. The intricate topography produces an ever-changing landscape. Vistas change dramatically from one moment to the next, which makes for wonderfully scenic backpacking, mostly above the timber line. Campsites are, typically, located beside lakes or in high cirques, separated by a day's hike to cross from one cirque to another. The length of time spent hiking is dictated by the cirque positions, which makes days well defined and often shorter than in other ranges. For this reason, the trek is best described on a day-by-day basis.

DAY 1 (*9.5km or 6 miles; 485m or 1600ft*) In a south-to-north direction the trek begins at Tin Cup Hiker trailhead on Pettit Lake and climbs the canyon of Pettit Lake Creek to Alice Lake (2620m; 8600ft). The ascent, mostly through forest of Douglas fir and lodgepole pine, is never without interest. Along the way there are waterfalls and a number of river crossings. The scenery becomes increasingly impressive, with the approach to Alice Lake itself

OPPOSITE INSET *The late evening sun reflects off the west face of El Capitan; this peak is favoured by rock climbers, who hang from its crevices overnight.*
OPPOSITE *Day five of the Sawtooth Trail climbs through natural rock gardens above Redfish canyon on the ascent from Flatrock Junction to Alpine Lake.*

TOP *Viewed from the lake in Temple basin, rock scenery towers above the Cramer Lakes – Sevy Peak is in the centre, with the Arrowhead to its right.*
ABOVE RIGHT *The west face of El Capitan, illuminated by late evening light, is reflected on the surface of a still pool near the entrance to Alice Lake.*

dominated by the great prow of El Capitan (3018m; 9901ft). Two ponds signal your arrival at the lake, whose beautifully wooded peninsulas and soaring rock peaks make it, perhaps, the most picturesque of all Sawtooth lakes. Pitch camp and settle in to watch the sunset show on El Capitan.

DAY 2 *(8km or 5 miles; 245m or 800ft)* Above Alice Lake the scenery is dominated by Snowyside Peak (3245m; 10,651ft). The trail climbs past the Twin Lakes to Snowyside Pass east of the mountain, then descends to another beautiful campsite beside the 'flower garden' shores of Toxaway Lake.

DAY 3 *(7km or 4.5 miles; 270m or 900ft)* A narrow pass north of Toxaway Lake enables the trail to cross a side ridge and reach Edna, one of a series of lakes clustered in the next cirque. The switchback ascent to the 2830m (9280ft) pass is easy, but the descent is steep. Days two and three could be combined into a single longer hike, but why rush amid such scenery?

DAY 4 *(10km or 6 miles; 395m or 1300ft)* Beyond Edna Lake the trail continues its descent through forest past Virginia Lake to the South Fork of the Payette River, which must be forded. The landscape then becomes more rugged as the trail climbs past Hidden Lake and above the timber line once more to reach the Cramer Divide (2890m; 9480ft) at the foot of the north-west ridge of the Temple, whose summit is topped by a precariously perched rock. From this highpoint of the trek, a 210m (700ft) descent of scree (and maybe snow) leads into the heart of Temple basin, a wonderfully wild bowl of rock tucked beneath the splintered northwest ridge of the Temple. The Temple's towers reflect in a perfectly positioned little lake. Hovering further round the cirque is the improbable blade of rock called the Arrowhead, one of the most incredible formations in the entire range. The ever-changing patterns of light in the basin may well persuade you to spend a rest day here. Alternatively, you may wish to camp further down at the Cramer Lakes to lessen the length of the following day's hike.

ABOVE *Lakeside meadows around Toxaway Lake, beneath the slopes of Snowyside Peak – the result is a highly picturesque campsite.*

ABOVE *Descending into Temple basin from the Cramer Divide. The trail is still covered by early season snow; note the balanced rock forming the Temple's summit.*

LOCATION The Rockies, south-central Idaho, USA.

WHEN TO GO End July to mid-September, although snow may be encountered on the north side of passes until mid-August.

START Tin Cup Hiker trailhead (2135m; 7000ft) on Pettit Lake, 29km (18 miles) south of Stanley.

FINISH Iron Creek trailhead and campground (2040m; 6700ft), 9km (6 miles) west of Stanley. For a small fee, commercial whitewater rafting companies in Stanley will drive your car from starting point to finishing trailhead.

DURATION 8–10 days (82km; 51 miles).

MAX. ALTITUDE The Cramer Divide (2900m; 9480ft).

TECHNICAL CONSIDERATIONS Excellent trail throughout, but a trek of this length and wildness should be attempted only by experienced backpackers. Snow obliterates high elevations of the trail in early season. The fording of several rivers is necessary.

EQUIPMENT Good boots, wet-weather gear, warm clothes, backpack, tent and sleeping gear, food and cooking utensils. Sunscreen and mosquito repellent.

TREKKING STYLE Backpacking, often above the timber line, with great views. Well-maintained trails and signposts. Camping necessary throughout. If there is a need to curtail the trek for any reason, many side trails provide easy escape routes.

PERMITS/RESTRICTIONS Access is unrestricted; no permits are required. Do make use of voluntary self-registration facilities at trailheads, as hiker counts influence trail budgets.

DANGERS Black bears have been known to annoy campers at trailhead campgrounds (but do not often venture into the high country); nevertheless, it is wise to cook and store food away from the tent. Streams may contain giardia. All drinking water should be boiled, filtered or treated with iodine.

MAPS Sawtooth Wilderness, Idaho, 1:48,000 by Earthwalk Press.

ABOVE Day one of the trail leads hikers up through fir and pine forests to stop for the night at Alice Lake, poised serenely at a height of 2620m (8600ft).

INFORMATION

Stanley Ranger Station, Star Route (5km/ 3 miles south of) Stanley, Idaho 83278; tel: +1-208-7743681.

SNRA Visitor Center, Star Route (13km/ 8 miles north of) Ketchum, Idaho 83340; tel: +1-208-7267672.

Stanley Chamber of Commerce, PO Box 59, Stanley, Idaho 83278; tel: +1-208-7743411.

Websites: www.stanleycc.org

www.fs.fed.us/r4/sawtooth

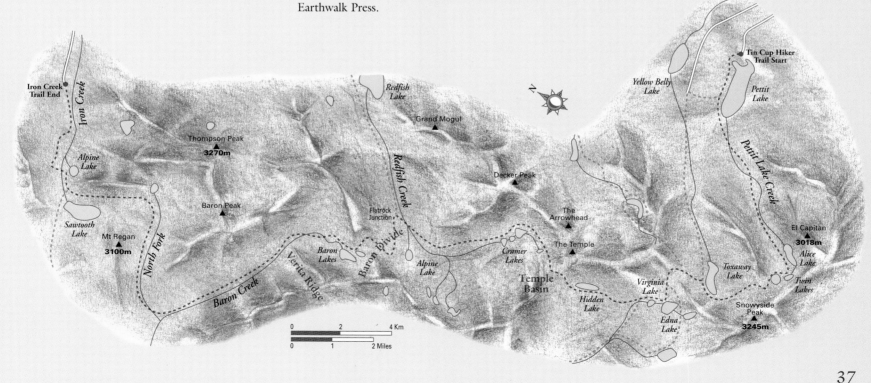

DAY 5 *(15km or 9.5 miles; 550m or 1800ft)* From Temple basin, a 150m (500ft) descent reaches the timber line at the three Cramer Lakes, where the trail passes the waterfall that feeds the middle lake, then crosses beautiful open parkland. Continuing down through forest, the route eventually reaches Redfish Creek at Flatrock Junction, a popular picnic spot and day-hike destination from Redfish Lake, 6km (4 miles) down a side canyon. The river is forded on the flat slabs that give the place its name, then the day's ascent begins, up via switchbacks through lush rock gardens where you will see Indian paintbrush, Wyoming's state flower. Alpine Lake is passed, with ever-widening views back to Temple basin, and the climb ends at a gap in the main ridge known as the Baron Divide (2790m; 9160ft). From here the three Baron Lakes can be seen cupped in a remote basin between the main ridge and the climbers' playground of Verita Ridge, which is crested with amazing rock formations such as El Pima, Damocles and the Leaning Tower of Pisa. Descend into the basin, camp beside one of the lakes and wonder at the splendour towering above you.

DAY 6 *(12km; 8 miles)* This easy trekking day is unusual in that it requires no uphill effort; instead the trail descends 850m (2800ft) beside tumbling Baron Creek to its junction with the North Fork of Baron Creek – at 1735m (5700ft) much lower than either the starting or finishing trailheads.

DAY 7 *(11km or 7 miles; 850m or 2800ft)* A tough ascent with one river crossing regains the height lost on the previous day, as the trail makes a long climb through luxurious vegetation beside the North Fork of Baron Creek to a rugged defile east of Mount Regan (3100m; 10,190ft). Beyond this lies Sawtooth Lake, the day's destination and a welcome sight. The picturesque lake lies in a rocky bowl beneath the imposing north face of Mount Regan and is the largest high lake in the Sawtooths. Ice floes can still be seen here in July.

DAY 8 *(8km or 5 miles)* The trail bids a sad farewell to the high country with another easy day that consists entirely of a descent beside Iron Creek, Sawtooth Lake's outlet stream. In a series of switchbacks, the trail twists down to the timber line at Alpine Lake (not the same as Day five's namesake), then continues down the curving Iron Creek valley. On the north side of the valley is one final, typically impressive 'tooth' ridge before the trail exits the mountains at Iron Creek trailhead.

OPPOSITE *The trail through the forest on the descent from the Cramer Lakes to Flatrock Junction – its name derived from the flattened rock wedges that litter the river.*

ABOVE *The North Fork of Baron Creek is one of several rivers on the Sawtooth Trail that need to be forded; this particular one occurs on day seven.*

TOP *In this reflection in Sawtooth Lake of the imposing north face of Mount Regan, rock, snow and water combine to form a magical vista.*

ALASKA ON FOOT
A Walk on the Wild·Side

The Back Yard Wilderness of Anchorage, Alaska
DEAN JAMES

Across the mirrored lake, the haunting call of a common loon broke the evening's silence. The bird's lonesome cry, similar to the eerie sound of the wolf, emphasized the true wilderness that encroached upon us. As night fell the deep forest that surrounded us seemed to close in ever further. In the growing darkness, we all felt the timeless spirit of Alaska, a peculiar mix of awe for this untamed land and an almost primeval fear of its vast emptiness.

Our group of seven had arrived in Alaska some days earlier on the incredibly scenic flight from Seattle to Anchorage. Directly south of that city, across Cook Inlet, the Kenai Peninsula juts out like a large thumb into the cold northern Pacific Ocean. Lying in the back yard of Alaska's main city, the Kenai has become a very popular recreational area, though it still holds on to its 'last frontier' atmosphere. The mountainous, heavily forested peninsula still boasts an impressive complement of wildlife: black and brown bear, wolf, moose, caribou, and wolverine, and has the most extensive trail system in the state. Probably the best known trek in Alaska is along the Resurrection Trail system, which is made up of three connecting routes: the Resurrection Pass, Russian Lakes and Resurrection River trails run for 116km (72 miles), traversing the entire Kenai Peninsula from north to south along its eastern side.

The trail follows abandoned old tracks blazed by the legion of gold prospectors who swarmed into this area during the Turnagain Arm Gold Rush of the 1890s. It starts near Hope, a small ghostly quiet town whose halcyon days ended with the dying gold rush. It was the route we had selected as a suitable first trek in Alaska.

Our first day was a short leg through deep spruce forest. Passing the occasional bear dropping along the trail we quickly realized that we were not the only ones who were using this solitary track – the only one for miles around. Nervously we made much noise, singing and clapping, probably so much so that there was no way we would get to see any wildlife at all. Our first night's wild camp was in a shaded forest beside Caribou Creek.

As is customary in Alaska we spent the evening eating and drinking around a campfire of dead logs.

The second day's trek led us higher, following the headwaters of Resurrection Creek. In the crystal-clear morning we had grand views through gradually thinning forest to the surrounding Kenai mountains. As we gained altitude, the trees became increasingly stunted until we reached the tree line and could venture out into open moorland. In unusually sunny weather for the area, it was wonderful to leave the claustrophobic forest behind and stride out over the

open landscape above. We made our way up to the main watershed at Resurrection Pass (792m; 2600ft), which was carpeted in juniper berries and fiery Indian paintbrush. On both sides of the pass were numerous small, beaver-dammed lakes, but unfortunately the dens were disused and we did not get to see the big-toothed, comical rodents. The 1200m (4000ft) mountains that flank the pass were covered in white reindeer moss, which appeared like fresh snow on the hillsides. We camped at the top of the pass, surrounded by hordes of noisy, whistling marmots and were treated to a rare sighting of a small herd of Kenai upland caribou that roamed the hillsides above us.

That evening three members of our group walked to a small lake nearby where they encountered a lone wolf who had come down to drink. For just a moment, they were quite close to the animal, which looked directly at them with its intense, intelligent eyes. Quite an experience and an incredibly rare one even for the Alaskan wilderness!

Over the next few days we descended from Resurrection Pass into and along the Juneau Creek valley with its beautiful tree-lined lakes. One night we camped in an idyllic position on the banks of Swan Lake near the head of the valley. The shallow sides of the lake were choked with dead or dying sockeye

INSET *Looking apprehensive at the start of the Resurrection River valley – and real bear country! This is the most difficult section of the entire trek.*
OPPOSITE *After setting up a wilderness camp in the Kenai mountains following a hard day's walking, it is time to relax and absorb the grandness of the view.*

TOP *A scarlet splash provided by the leaves of the Bearberry* (Arctostaphylos uva-ursi)*, a shrub known locally as the Kinnikinnick bush.*
ABOVE RIGHT *Where migrating fish swim upstream to spawn, bald eagles find a ready supply of protein in Alaska's remote wilderness.*

salmon, which, after their amazing journey from the ocean and up the creek's rapids, had arrived back in the lake to spawn. This natural occurrence is part of a three-year cycle – in summer, the salmon return to the lake where they first hatched; here they spawn, after which they die. Their young then move downstream and out to sea. They will return three years later to repeat the cycle.

That evening, as the last colours faded away and darkness fell, a large female moose quietly left the forest and entered the lake. She looked down her long nose at us for quite some time before lifting her incredibly long legs to splash off across the lake and into the night. Soon it was totally dark and our imagination turned to the fresh bear droppings, huge paw prints and claw scratch-marks on trees we had seen earlier in the day. A little nervous, we made our last toilet stops before retiring.

Descending the Juneau Creek valley the following day, we again entered deep forest and came across large areas of the infamous devil's club. This forest shrub grows to 2m (7ft) in height and forms an impenetrable undergrowth especially along

riverbanks. Its extremely nutritious leaves are protected by inch-long brittle spines that break off when you brush against them and can easily penetrate the skin. Stories of exploration in Alaska are littered with epics about this evil-looking plant. Eventually the Juneau Creek valley opens out into the impressive Kenai valley. We crossed the deep turquoise Kenai River where the Sterling Highway conveniently bridges it. It felt quite strange to emerge from the solitude of the forest and stride out onto the wide, hard tarmac road. We had only been in the wilderness for five days but the contrast was striking. Large American pick-ups and motor homes whizzing past made us feel like strange, scruffy intruders.

On the south side of the Kenai River we booked into the official Russian River Campground, where, as previously arranged, a transit van from Anchorage arrived to replenish our supplies for the last part of our trip.

The following morning we again headed southwards into the wilderness, this time following the Russian Lakes Trail. Numerous moose loomed

ABOVE *Early autumn (fall) in the Kenai mountains is characterized by slopes carpeted with red Alpine Bearberry, another* Arctostaphylos *species.*

LEFT *The devil's club* (Echinopanax horridum).
ABOVE RIGHT *A section of trail closed to the public due to recent bear activity in Resurrection River valley.*

LOCATION Kenai Peninsula, Chugach National Forest, southern Alaska.

WHEN TO GO May to October (best time is autumn (last week August/first week September).

START Resurrection Pass trailhead near Hope, Kenai Peninsula. No public transport to Hope. For ground transportation from Anchorage to the various outlying areas, contact: Earth Tours (Bill Merchant), 1001 W. 12th Avenue, Anchorage, Alaska 99501; tel: +907-2799907; e-mail: earthtrs@alaska.net

FINISH Exit Glacier near Seward, southern Kenai Peninsula. Daily bus and train services from Anchorage to Seward in summer.

DURATION 5–7 days (116km; 72 miles).

MAX. ALTITUDE Resurrection Pass (792m; 2600ft).

TECHNICAL CONSIDERATIONS Moderate fitness level required. Good unmarked route except for Resurrection River Trail (final 25km; 16 miles), which is often overgrown with possible difficult river crossings. No climbing necessary.

EQUIPMENT Sturdy boots, warm clothes, wet-weather gear, backpack, tent, sleeping bag and mat, food and cooking utensils, insect repellent.

TREKKING STYLE Backpacking. Several huts en route run by US Forest Service. Camping at numerous maintained wild sites near huts and at points between.

PERMITS/RESTRICTIONS None required. No camping restrictions in Chugach National Forest.

DANGERS Be alert when travelling through bear country. Make noise, particularly where visibility is limited, to let bears know you are there. Never approach bears, but maintain minimum safe distance of at least 100m (330ft), especially from sow with young. When camping, sleep in a tent. Separate food, cooking, and sleeping areas by at least 100m. Store food in bear-resistant containers or suspend in trees 3m (10ft) above ground.

River crossings can be tricky. Ford glacial rivers in the early morning when water level is lowest. Never go barefoot and don't cross with bare legs. Cross as a group, linking arms or holding a stick horizontally. Loosen backpack straps and undo waist belt so you can drop it if you fall.

Mosquitoes are so large hereabouts, they are often referred to as the 'national bird of Alaska'. Numbers peak in late June.

MAPS REQUIRED USGS (United States Geological Survey) 1:63,360; 2 sheets for northern part of trek: Seward (D-8) and Seward (C-8) quads. Southern half of trek covered by Trails Illustrated topographical map ca. 1:100,000; sheet 231, Kenai Fiords National Park.

INFORMATION

Alaska Division of Tourism, PO Box 110801, Juneau, AK 99811; tel: +1-907-4652010. Mountaineering Club of Alaska, PO Box 102037, Anchorage, AK 99510; tel: +1-907-2721811. Alaska Public Lands Information Centre, 605 West 4th Avenue, Anchorage, Alaska 99501; tel: +1-907-2712737 (this office handles all the information for Alaska's national parks). Website: alaskan.com (Alaska in general) e-mail: mca@alaska.net

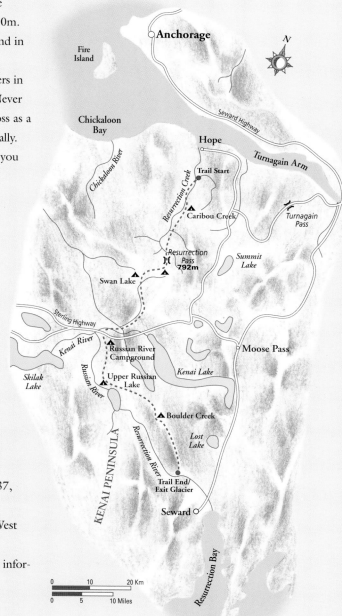

out of the banks of valley cloud that shrouded the forest in a damp, quiet mist. That night we camped on the wild shore of the Upper Russian Lake.

As we turned in for the night, dark sinister clouds were rolling in from the vast Harding Icefield to the south. The wind picked up and churned the lake into a mass of mares' tails. The forest swayed and creaked ominously. Only two of us remained outside the tents as twilight faded, chatting quietly about the approaching storm. Just then, a wolverine sauntered right through our camp, quite nonchalantly, not even bothering to look sideways at us, sitting frozen to the spot. This badger-sized member of the weasel family has a fearsome reputation in Alaska. It is claimed that even grizzly bears will give way when they encounter a wolverine. Apprehensively we said goodnight, retired to our tents and lay listening to the wind ... until we distinctly heard one of our cooking pots being moved outside. Through the slightest gap in the fly sheet I peered

into the blackness, and there – very close to the tent – was the unmistakable humpbacked silhouette of a grizzly. The huge jet-black form moved through our camp and to the lake from where one could still hear the frantic splashing of spawning salmon. After what seemed like an age of holding our breath, the bear moved away, probably far more interested in a protein-rich salmon meal.

The last leg of our walk, along the Resurrection River, was the hardest part: various bridges had been washed away, leaving potentially awkward river crossings. Innumerable trees had fallen across the track forming difficult obstacles for backpackers. It was with some relief, therefore, that we crossed the last major creek by way of a log jam before again emerging from the forest onto the gravel Exit Glacier Road. As we ambled contentedly towards the snout of the Exit Glacier and the end of our trip, I stared off into the wilderness; I had already begun to plan my next journey to 'Alaska, the Last Frontier'.

OPPOSITE *This early September scene – the forest tinged by autumn and the high peaks cloaked with first winter snows – is very typical of the Alaskan landscape.*

ABOVE *Negotiating a crossing of the Resurrection River; the waters are incredibly cold as the rivers here are fed from thawing glaciers nearby.*

CONTINENTAL DIVIDE TRAIL

Along the spine of the Rockies

Rockies from Canada to New Mexico, Western USA
CHRIS TOWNSEND

The idea for a Canada-to-Mexico walking route – following the Rocky mountain watershed of North America – first occurred to Benton Mackaye (founder of the Appalachian Trail) in 1966 and the US Congress authorized a study of the trail under the National Trails System Act of 1968. Five years later, a hiker named Jim Wolf walked through northern Montana and, independently, envisioned a trail along the length of the Continental Divide. Since then, he has worked tirelessly to realize his vision. In 1978 came the designation as a National Scenic Trail by Congress; in the same year, Wolf founded the Continental Divide Trail Society, dedicated to the planning, development and maintenance of the path. Today it is one of the world's premier long-distance trails.

The 5000km (3100-mile) length of the Continental Divide Trail (CDT) takes in a great sweep of the American West (though only the 1282km [795-mile] section from Canada through Montana and Idaho to Yellowstone National Park is officially designated). It encompasses the dark, remote forests and dramatic mountains of the Northern Rockies and leads through the desert heart of Wyoming to the rolling heights of the Colorado Rockies and multi-coloured desert mesas of New Mexico. A difference of nearly 20 degrees in latitude between the northern and southern trail-ends results in a noticeable difference in climate and ecosystems: in Montana the timber line is 2700m (8800ft), in New Mexico it is 3600m (11,800ft). Most of the trail is above 2000m (6500ft) with the highest section occurring in Colorado, where it lies above 3000m (10,000ft) for many miles. Much of the Divide Trail lies in pristine wilderness, but it also passes through ranchland, logging and mining areas, and Indian reservations. Along the way, there is much history that unfolds from the tracks of westbound wagon trains on the Oregon Trail in Wyoming to Anasazi ruins and Mogollon cliff dwellings in New Mexico.

The first Europeans to cross the northern part of the Divide were Meriwether Lewis and William Clark in 1805 on their expedition across the continent to the Pacific Ocean. The southern Divide was reached much earlier – the

Spanish left inscriptions in the soft sandstone of El Morro (Inscription Rock, New Mexico) in the 1500s.

A through-hike of the CDT is a major undertaking as the trail is only 70 per cent complete. Snow is likely in the mountains at some point – southbounders will probably have to deal with it at the start of the trail in Glacier National Park and possibly again in southern Colorado, while those heading northwards are likely to encounter snow in southern Colorado and then have to hope they can make it through the Northern Rockies before the autumn snows set in. Whereas northbound walkers have easy, flat terrain at the beginning of their journey, heading south does mean starting in very rugged terrain. However, New Mexico can be hiked late in the year, unlike the Northern Rockies. Overall, moving south is possibly the easier direction. Jim Wolf's excellent guidebooks describe the route in this way; it is also the direction this writer took in the route described here.

The CDT begins in Glacier National Park, a very rugged, spectacular part of the Northern Rockies where snow lies much of the year. The trail stays high on the steep mountain slopes, below the jagged crest along which the Divide itself runs. South of the park it enters the largest roadless area in the USA outside of Alaska, passing through the Bob Marshall and Scapegoat wildernesses.

In the former, the trail runs below the impressive Chinese Wall, a limestone cliff that stretches for mile after mile, towering 300m (1000ft) above the forest. Most of the walking here is in forest and there are many creek fords, which can be difficult and potentially dangerous early on in the season when

OPPOSITE INSET *The Gila Cliff dwellings in southern New Mexico were built in the 13th century by the Mogollon people, but were abandoned after only 40 years.*
OPPOSITE *The trail runs for several miles through Douglas fir forest above the serenely beautiful St Mary's Lake, in Glacier National Park.*

TOP *This view south along the Divide, from James Peak in the Colorado Rockies, is the highest section of the entire trail.*
ABOVE RIGHT *A trekker leaves behind the Chinese wall, a 300m (1000ft) limestone cliff in the Bob Marshall Wilderness, in the state of Montana.*

the previous winter's snow is still in the process of melting. Scapegoat Wilderness is drier, more open and allows easier progress.

Gentler terrain continues beyond the wilderness areas and the trail often runs along the Divide itself in central Montana, following a line of rounded hills. Once past the town of Butte, the CDT changes direction and heads west as it begins a loop around the Big Hole, the westernmost valley of the Mississippi-Missouri river system. Here the landscape changes as the trail enters the beautiful alpine country of the Anaconda-Pintler Wilderness with its many scenic timber-line lakes.

The route turns back south at Lost Trail Pass, on the border with Idaho, where Lewis and Clark crossed the Divide. Walking through the splendid Bitterroot mountains is tough and resupply points are far apart and a long way from the trail, but the scenic rewards are great in this pristine wilderness with its alpine peaks, crystal-clear lakes and flower meadows.

The terrain eases off as the route turns eastwards and follows the Divide across rolling hills grazed by large herds of cattle. The grassland gives way to the Centennial mountains, a sloping tableland of sedimentary rock cliffs, meadows and forest groves.

Beyond the Centennials, the trail reaches Wyoming and world-famous Yellowstone National Park. The route now leads mostly through undulating lodgepole-pine forest where bubbling hot pools, geysers and other thermal features add interest.

The landscape becomes more exciting as the park is left for the Teton Wilderness, a region of deep, glaciated valleys rimmed by massive, brightly coloured cliffs. Here, too, is the Parting of the Waters, where small North Two Ocean Creek splits, the eastern branch running some 5600km (3500 miles) to the Atlantic Ocean and the western branch 2200km (1350 miles) to the Pacific. Higher mountains are reached in the magnificent Wind River range, the final glorious flourish of the Northern Rockies where the trail lies mostly above 3050m (10,000ft).

In the Montana and Wyoming Rockies the trail is usually high in the mountains, leading through montane and subalpine zones. Below the timber line are huge coniferous forests where lodgepole pine dominates, with stands of massive Douglas fir in shady places. Approaching the timber line the most common trees are Engelmann spruce, subalpine fir and occasional stands of subalpine larch, which turns a glorious orange in autumn. At lower levels, stands of quaking aspen can be found – another tree that gives spectacular autumn colours – along with black cottonwoods beside water.

Alders, willows, cherries and maples and a mass of different shrubs grow in clearings and avalanche paths. These are an attractive sight, especially when in

ABOVE *The remotest section of the Continental Divide Trail works its way through the complex tangle of mountains of the Bob Marshall Wilderness.*

flower or in autumn colours, but if you lose the trail and have to fight your way through the tangle you'll end up cursing them. Many wildflowers grow in the mountains and if you happen to be hiking in July or August, a flower guide would come in handy.

Around 60 species of mammals occur in the Northern Rockies, but hikers are unlikely to see more than deer. In the southern part of the region, moose inhabit the damper areas and can be seen in marshes and shallow lakes at dawn and dusk. On cliffs above the timber line live shaggy, white mountain goats. Bighorn sheep, too, may be seen high in the mountains.

The most dramatic animals are, of course, bears. Black bears occur throughout the region, with grizzlies in Glacier and Yellowstone national parks and the Bob Marshall and Teton wilderness areas. At dawn and dusk, coyotes are more likely to be heard than seen.

Red squirrels are common throughout the forest and often chatter loudly at passing hikers. Various ground squirrels and chipmunks may also be spotted. In boulder fields, hoary marmots sunbathing on rocks whistle loudly when alarmed – as do the smaller picas that also dwell in rock piles. Porcupines sometimes wander into camp and try to eat boots or articles of clothing (because of their salt content). A stick is useful for driving them away – you don't want to get too close! Beavers are seldom seen, but their dams and lodges are found on many slow-moving creeks and rivers.

Although many birds live in the Northern Rockies they mostly remain hidden in the forest. Likely to be seen around campsites, in the hope of finding food scraps, are gray jays and Clark's nutcrackers. Spruce grouse, various woodpeckers, smaller finches and sparrows are common. Above the timber line ravens may be seen soaring overhead, as well as red-tailed hawks and, just maybe, a golden eagle.

South of the Wind Rivers there's a sudden and dramatic change as the route descends to the Great Divide basin. Here, the Divide splits to embrace this waterless desert area. (The trail isn't marked or complete here and some road walking is necessary.) The Great Divide basin is sagebrush country, home to wild horses and the fast–running pronghorn, a graceful deer-like animal.

ABOVE *The mountain goat symbolizes the northern Rockies; these goats are good climbers, well adapted to the cliffs and steep terrain.*
LEFT *Halfmoon Creek in Colorado's Sawatch range separates the highest peaks of the Rocky mountains – Mounts Elbert and Massive.*

South of the Great Divide basin the trail slowly climbs through the Sierra Madre mountains, out of Wyoming and into the Colorado Rockies, a complex area of small, high mountain ranges. The trail is marked and maintained through most of Colorado. From the Mount Zirkel Wilderness it passes through the ranges named Park, Rabbits Ears and Never Summer, touches the edge of Rocky Mountain National Park and then continues south through the Indian Peaks Wilderness and along the crest of the Front range, the highest part of the trail. After this it skirts the two highest of the Rocky mountain peaks: Elbert (4395m; 14,421ft) and Massive (4399m; 14,433ft), both of which can easily be climbed. The CDT in Colorado finishes with a long circuit around the head of the Rio Grande valley in the superb rugged San Juan mountains and the Weminuche Wilderness.

The fauna and flora of the Colorado Rockies is similar to that of the Northern Rockies though there are no grizzly bears here, which may be a relief to some. In early summer, mountain and forest meadows put on a rich display of flowers, while in autumn various shrubs, along with aspen trees, glow bright red and yellow against the dark green of the conifers.

Coming down from the San Juan mountains the trail enters its last state, New Mexico, where walking is mostly across open sagebrush-dotted desert with expansive vistas and huge skyscapes. Much of the route is on dirt roads. Highlights are the massive Chaco Mesa, a complex plateau lined with steep cliffs, the shady wooded ridges of the Zuni mountains and El Morro National Monument. Straggly, spiky bushes and plants dot the desert, tearing at clothes and skin, while long green strands of cottonwoods and willows line the few watercourses. In the higher semidesert areas such as Chaco Mesa, small pinon pine and juniper bushes cover the land.

Not far from the finish, the terrain changes again as the trail climbs into the Gila National Forest and back into montane forest of big conifers and aspens, including some fine ponderosa pine. An optional route goes via the Gila Cliff Dwellings, cut high into a cliff. South of the Gila National Forest, dirt roads lead across the final stretch of desert to either Antelope Wells or Columbus, the two possible finishing points. Once at the border, you can turn and stare northwards over the desert, imagining the Divide stretching out to Canada, and memorizing the exquisite landscapes and adventures along the way.

ABOVE *The highest mountains along the Divide occur in the Sawatch mountain range, cloaked here in aspens. Seven of its summits tower over 4300m (14,000ft).*

OPPOSITE *A spectacular view north along the Divide, seen across a camp high on the slopes of James Peak in the Front Range, Colorado.*

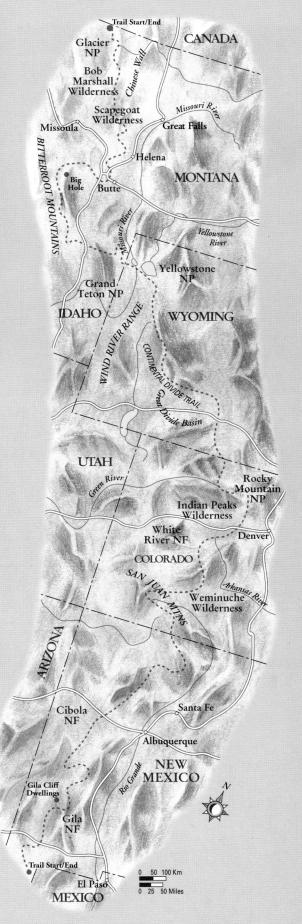

LOCATION The length of the Rocky mountains, from Canada to New Mexico, USA.

WHEN TO GO North–south: late June to November; south-north: late April to October. Hiking the CDT over two or more seasons is easier: mid-July to mid-September is the best time for Montana, Wyoming and Colorado; spring or autumn (March to May and October to November respectively) are best for New Mexico.

START/FINISH South: Antelope Wells or Columbus (New Mexico); north: Glacier National Park (Montana) or Waterton Lakes National Park (Alberta). Post offices in Lincoln (Montana), Tendoy and Leadore (Idaho) keep registers for CDT hikers. These serve merely as a record, and filling them in is not compulsory.

DURATION 4–6 months (5000km; 3100 miles).

MAX. ALTITUDE The Front Range's Parry Peak, Colorado (4081m; 13,391ft).

TECHNICAL CONSIDERATIONS A trail for experienced backpackers with good navigation skills as there are no markings in places. Some very steep and rough sections. Some dry sections where water must be carried. Resupply points are far apart; food for a week or more will often have to be carried.

The weather is hot and dry in the deserts; warm in the mountains with afternoon thunderstorms. There is snow in autumn and winter.

EQUIPMENT Hiking footwear, backpack, tent or tarp, sleeping bag rated to -5/-10°C (23–14°F), food and cooking utensils, warm clothes, rain gear. A GPS (Global Positioning System receiver) is useful.

TREKKING STYLE Backpacking. Camping essential.

PERMITS/RESTRICTIONS Wilderness permits are needed for Glacier and Yellowstone national parks and for some wilderness areas. Contact the CDTS or CDTA (see below) for the latest information.

DANGERS Black bears occur in many areas. In most places they are not a problem, but obtaining up-to-date information from rangers is advisable. Grizzly bears occur in the Teton Wilderness and Yellowstone National Park in Wyoming, plus Glacier National Park and the Bob Marshall Wilderness in Montana. Although encounters are unlikely, precautions must be taken. Bigger threats are stream crossings, lightning, falling off a cliff, injury in a remote area and hypothermia – usual rugged wilderness hazards.

INFORMATION

Continental Divide Trail Society, 3704 North Charles Street #601, Baltimore, MD 21218, USA.

Website: www.gorp.com/cdts

e-mail: cdtsociety@aol.com

Continental Divide Trail Alliance, PO Box 628, Pine, CO 80470, USA.

Website: www.cdtrail.org; e-mail: cdnst@aol.com

EXPLORADORES VALLEY
Fording icy Patagonian meltwaters

Carlos Ibanez del Campo Province, Chile, South America

DAVE WILLIS

Most visitors to Chile are drawn to the Atacama Desert, Puerto Montt or Torres del Paine National Park. Others choose to discover the lakes and glaciers of the Laguna San Rafael National Park in the province known as Carlos Ibanez del Campo, or simply Region 11, because it is here that the truly adventurous traveller will find some of the most outstanding and demanding treks in the country.

This area of northern Patagonia lies at the junction of three tectonic plates and is very important geologically as it produces earthquakes and volcanoes in abundance. Most of the tremors are too slight to be noticed though sensitive instruments record one every 20 minutes. (While we were here, a large volcano erupted and devastated an area of over 130km² [50 square miles].) The fact that only a handful of farming families lives here means that most seismic activity goes unreported.

Rainfall is high in this temperate zone. Storms sweep in frequently from the western Pacific and the plants evidently love it. Vast stretches of virgin rainforest, glaciated valleys and mountains make up this largely unexplored wilderness, offering an almost limitless supply of possibilities. The Exploradores valley is one of them.

In the mid-1970s, the Río Exploradores was surveyed as a possible road link to the coast. The road was never built, but a path of sorts was hacked out which these days, though overgrown and sketchy, still serves as a horse track for local farmers. Many of the old, blue-painted survey markers can still be found, rotting in the dense forest undergrowth.

OPPOSITE INSET *Yet another crossing required: the Río Norte is affected by glacial meltwater from the Campo de Hielo Norte, causing levels to rise and fall quickly.*
OPPOSITE *Puerto Ibanez, one of the small ports tucked into the shoreline of the scenically splendid Lago General Carrera.*
TOP *Campo de Hielo Norte (the Northern Icefield) is clearly visible from the lake.*
ABOVE RIGHT *Dr Ruth Murdy of the UK conducts a geological seismic survey on the banks of the Exploradores – a highly active region of earthquake activity, although most events are only detectable using sensitive equipment.*
PREVIOUS PAGES *The Inca site of Machu Picchu is the culmination of a trek on a restored ancient road, the Inca Trail, which crosses three staggeringly high passes.*

The route described below follows the river valleys of the Río Norte, Río Circo and Río Exploradores. Camping takes place in the wild, beside the river, with abundant supplies of fallen timber for firewood. The route starts from Puerto Tranquilo on the shores of the Lago General Carrera where supplies can be bought and advice about the trek can be sought from the locals at the Campo Lindo store. The distance of 90km (56 miles) to the Golfo de Elefantes should take nine days to complete. This narrow sea channel, which separates the Taitao Peninsula from the mainland was named not after elephants, but the elephant seals that frequent this inlet in summer.

Leaving the road, the surveyed path is soon found on the heavily silted riverbank that is dotted with dead and waterlogged trees. Although a bit heavy underfoot and with occasional sinking into muddy silt, it is easily followed. (Our only complaint was the weight of our backpacks. Mine weighed 19kg, or 42lb – nine days' ration packs at 1kg, or 2lb, each plus my gear.)

By day two the valley narrows, hemmed in by steep cliffs with thickening shrubs and small trees along the riverbank. After a while, the survey path turns abruptly into the now deeper and swifter flowing river to re-emerge on the opposite bank. Since crags bar the way ahead, there is no choice but to wade across. The river carries glacial meltwater and is very, very cold. Suddenly the reality of this wilderness trek becomes apparent: there will be no bridges, safe crossings or easy rescue. (River crossings are the most dangerous things backpackers have to contend with. During the course of our week-long trek we would cross and re-cross many times, each time making a fire afterwards to dry our clothes and warm up. This is no place to get hypothermia!)

Every mountainside and valley is cloaked in unbelievably dense tree growth and soon the forest encroaches right down to the riverbank. On the south side of the river, the path disappears into bottomless undergrowth and progress involves clambering over, through, under, and along broken and fallen stumps and tree trunks while searching for the next faded-blue marker. All the locals carry machetes and so should you. Forward progress is especially difficult through solid walls of, surprisingly, bamboo.

On day four the track emerges from the tangle onto a broad path skirting the edge of the Río Norte, which has now widened considerably. Clambering and struggling gives way to very pleasant walking with views of the high mountains towering above a widening valley ahead. Almost none of these peaks is named on maps, probably because few of them have been climbed. The approach through the dense forest is extremely difficult.

Lago Bayo, where the Río Norte turns into the Río Circo, is the first real landmark. Lakes always look picturesque, but here, so far from civilization and its distractions, the sense of peace and tranquillity is tangible. The occasional crumbling survey posts, last touched over 30 years ago, seem to be the only indication that anyone else has been here before. In reality, occasional *huasos* (cowboys) pass this way on horseback, tending whatever livestock they have.

The sense of untamed remoteness is reinforced by encounters with wildlife. Circling condors are a daily sight, their massive scale hard to appreciate when they wheel overhead at great altitude. Fish owls, too, are seen occasionally and you may even find fresh puma scat. However, the chances of actually seeing this incredibly shy and beautiful cat are so remote you could spend a lifetime trying to find one.

After Lago Bayo the river reaches a confluence that the locals call Río Deshielo. (When we were here, meltwater from the distant snowy peaks of the Campo de Hielo Norte, the Northern Icefield, had swollen this junction of three rivers to an impassable size and there was real concern that we would not be able to continue. Fortunately, we managed to cross safely at five o'clock the next morning, breaking the layer of ice on the surface as we went, before the sun had had a chance to increase the flow of meltwater yet again.) Conditions improve considerably from this point. Sandy beaches and silt washed up by the river make a pleasant walking surface, but the Río Circo becomes increasingly treacherous to cross.

Further downriver, the Circo becomes the Río Exploradores. It expands into a wide, deep channel as it approaches the coast. There is one more crossing at a farm called Teresa, but being close to the coast, this end of the Río Exploradores is more heavily frequented than the upstream reaches and offers the luxury of a simple pulley-line-and-boat ferry system.

On day nine, if you are on schedule, you should reach the coast after a pleasant walk through bamboo and thinning undergrowth beside the river. The point about being on schedule is a serious one, because there is only one way to get back from here – by boat – unless you want to turn around and retrace your route. (Be sure to organize your passage in advance, because it is only a resupply vessel for local farmers. Fortunately, these things are easily arranged with the local boatmen.)

The satisfaction of having traversed the length of the Exploradores valley from source to sea, to have made the effort and endured the hardships, doubles the pleasure of experiencing this pristine environment. Certainly, that's how I felt, motoring up the Golfo de Elefantes to head for the next adventure in this Patagonian Wilderness.

RIGHT *Guide ropes have been rigged here to aid a crossing of the fast-running Río Norte near Lago Bayo; a camp fire is often necessary afterwards to warm up.*

LOCATION Lago General Carrera, Northern Patagonia, Chile.

WHEN TO GO September to May, but high summer (January) will ensure the warmest weather and least rainfall.

START Puerto Tranquilo on the road from Coihaique to Cochrane. This is the Carretera (Highway) 7, or *Longitudinal Austral*, the only road south through Chile. Most travellers will start and finish their trip in Puerto Aisén where there is an airport and a coastal ferry service from Santiago. Puerto Tranquilo can be reached from Puerto Aisén either by bus or taxi.

FINISH Golfo de Elefantes. A resupply boat comes here once a week. Check on which day and arrange your return passage to Puerto Aisén in advance (book in Puerto Aisén).

DURATION 9 days (90km; 56 miles).

MAX. ALTITUDE All at about sea level.

TECHNICAL CONSIDERATIONS This is a wilderness trek with little or no backup available, suitable only for experienced, fit teams with good self-sufficiency skills. River crossing experience is essential.

In rural Chile, it is normal practice to send messages through the local radio station. Farmers who tend their livestock in remote valleys during the summer months stay in touch with their families in this way and most of them listen to the broadcasts as a matter of course. (In Puerto Tranquilo we sent a message via Radio Santa Maria to a local farmer who was willing to take us across the Río Circo on his horses. Unfortunately, the plan fell apart during the night when his tough little ponies escaped and crossed the river to graze on the far side!)

EQUIPMENT You will need to carry all food, cooking and camping equipment, and safety gear with you, including fire-starting materials, machete, static ropes (for river crossings) and an emergency radio. There is no chance of resupply once you leave the road. Wet-weather gear is essential. Line the inside of backpacks with canoeing-type dry-bags to protect the contents during river crossings.

TREKKING STYLE Backpacking, jungle trek. The track, vague and unrecognizable in parts, requires a considered approach but little navigation. Mostly wild camping; occasional abandoned timber shacks provide shelter. To reduce the weight of your pack, use bivvy bags and 'basher'-type shelters rather than heavy tents.

PERMITS AND RESTRICTIONS None at present. You will require a visa for Chile, and should inform the local carabíneros (police) where you are going.

MAPS REQUIRED Maps are available from the Chilean geographical authority in Santiago (Instituto Geografico Militar), Nueva Sta., Isobel No. 1640.

INFORMATION

To/from Coihaique: ferries, tel: 21971; buses, tel: 22987; air taxi, tel: 21172.

Southern Summits (outdoor pursuits operator), Merced 102–106, Casilla 1045 (22), Santiago; tel: +56-2-337784.

Websites: www.samexplo.org; www.latinworld.com

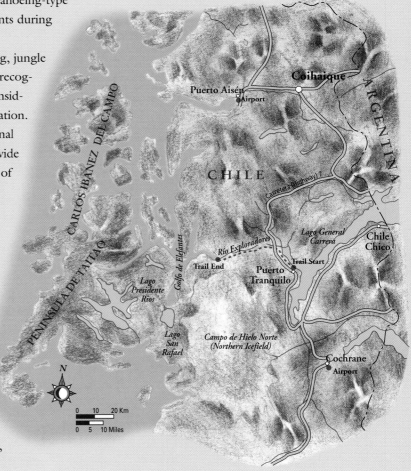

OPPOSITE *Nearing Lago Bayo, the forest thins into more open ground, making it easier for tired trekkers to find suitable sites to camp in at the end of the day.*

ABOVE *A male Patagonian sea lion,* Otaria byronia, *can weigh up to 300kg (662lb). Females weigh about half that and pups range between 10–15kg (22–33lb).*

INCA TRAIL
In the Footsteps of the Inca

Andean range, Peru, South America

DAVE WYNNE-JONES

The Inca Trail is world famous as a high-altitude trek through staggering Andean scenery. It follows a restored Inca road over three high passes with superb views of adjacent snowcapped Nevados and the Cordillera Vilcabamba, finally arriving at the ruined city of Machu Picchu.

The terrain includes high *puna* (cold, dry Andean grassland and scrub), rock outcrops, valleys cut by swift-flowing streams, lakes and marshes, eerie cloud forest and the cleared spaces of an ancient city centre. There's not much chance of seeing the endangered spectacled bear or tapir, but llama, the rabbit-like *viscachas*, hummingbirds, torrent ducks, birds of prey (even condors), and lots of butterflies and wildflowers are almost guaranteed.

A wilderness experience it isn't. *Campesino* farmers till the land around the villages, rangers patrol the route, and while the trail is big enough to accommodate the numbers, campsites may be crowded during the busiest months (June and July). Rather, it is an adventure – of the mind, as well as the body – centred on the intriguing and atmospheric Inca ruins along the way.

The Incas were preceded by various civilizations, but none managed to establish such a vast and powerful empire, in the space of just 100 years, before the Spaniards arrived. Since the Incas had no writing, all we know of their history was recorded by Spanish priests from the memories of those who survived the conquest. Much remains a mystery. Archaeologists theorize about the ruins, but no one has yet managed to explain how such incredibly fine stonework was constructed with tools made of copper.

The Inca Trail owes its existence to Hiram Bingham, a Yale historian who became an archaeologist after encountering Inca remains on a visit to Peru. He returned to discover the Machu Picchu site in 1911 and spent several years clearing the ruins and tracing roads that linked the city with other settlements. Luis Valcarcel in 1934, and Paul Frejos between 1940 and 1942, made further discoveries. Bingham would return in 1948 to inaugurate the highway link that bears his name from Puente Ruinas railway station to Machu Picchu.

Postwar development of international tourism has seen the area progress through national park status to become a UNESCO World Heritage Site today.

Walking through a fascinating landscape and taking time out to explore the ruins, developing your own theories or just soaking up the atmosphere, are the unique attractions of the Inca Trail. Altitude is the main problem and it's advisable first to spend a few days in and around Cuzco (3360m; 11,000ft), exploring the city's markets, museums and nearby ruins.

For an easier first day's hiking, start the Inca Trail from Chilca at Km 77, or the roadhead at Km 82, walk along the Urubamba River valley and spend the first night near Llaqtapata. Otherwise, take the local train to Km 88 (tourist trains don't stop there) and pay your park fees. After crossing the bridge there's a choice: either turn right for a quick visit to Tarapata first, or turn left and walk a dusty riverside track through eucalypts to reach Llaqtapata.

It's easy to dismiss Llaqtapata as just a collection of terraces, but looking down from a rock wall barring the way ahead, the full extent of these ruins is revealed. The path climbs steeply to the crest of the rise, where the Río Kusichaca has cut a deep little gorge, then it follows the river, gently gaining height, to Wayllabamba at 2750m (9020ft). Looking back, snowcapped Nevado Veronica can be seen towering above the valley.

Wayllabamba has a campsite, but further up the valley of the Río Llullucha are safer alternatives (theft is a problem) – at Tres Piedras, where the tributary Chaupiwayoq joins the Llullucha or any one of the small sites among the trees beyond. At 3600m (11,800ft), the campsite at Llulluchapampa, where lush polylepsis cloud forest gives way to open hillside, isn't very much higher than Cuzco for a first night on the trail and has a better early morning outlook.

OPPOSITE INSET *The llamas at Machu Picchu, so accustomed to the steady throngs of tourists, have learnt to pose for the cameras!*
OPPOSITE *The altitude at which the Runkurakay ruins, or Egg Fort, lie afford stupendous views back to Dead Woman's Pass and the Paqamayo valley.*

TOP *The Inca ruins are the remnants of a highly complex ancient civilization, based in Peru, that existed from 1100 to the Spanish conquest of the early 1530s.*
ABOVE RIGHT *The local Quechua Indians have a vibrant, living culture in which rich, colourful textiles and Andean music feature strongly.*

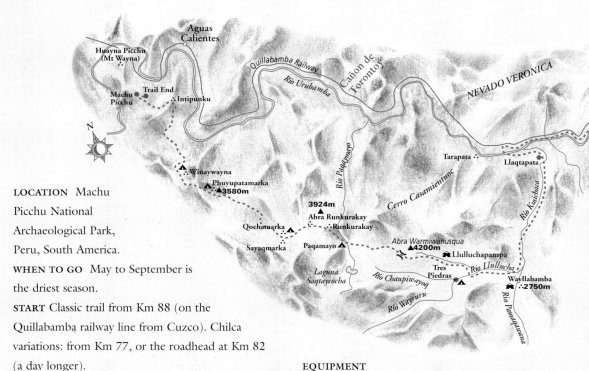

LOCATION Machu
Picchu National
Archaeological Park,
Peru, South America.

WHEN TO GO May to September is
the driest season.

START Classic trail from Km 88 (on the
Quillabamba railway line from Cuzco). Chilca
variations: from Km 77, or the roadhead at Km 82
(a day longer).

Finish Machu Picchu (bus to Agua Calientes for
train back to Cuzco).

DURATION 3–5 days (43 km; 27 miles).

MAX. ALTITUDE Abra Warmiwanusqua (4200m;
13,780ft), but most of the route is over 3000m
(9800ft) with two more high passes.

TECHNICAL CONSIDERATIONS Acclimatization to
altitude is essential. The trail requires no climbing or
scrambling. Carry your litter out with you to protect
the environment, and bury ablutory waste well away
from the trail or water.

EQUIPMENT

Boots, backpack, lightweight
tent, three-season sleeping bag and mat, stove, pans
and food, layers of clothing from thermal vest and
shorts to fleece pants and jacket, warm hat and
gloves, wet-weather gear, sun hat and cream, medical
kit, iodine tablets to sterilize water. Ski poles help ease
steep descents. It's worth taking a petrol stove as well
as a butane/propane *gaz* one. The small blue *gaz* car-
tridges are often available, but supplies cannot be
guaranteed. *Benzina blanca* (white gas) can always be
bought at chemists or *ferretaria* (ironmongers).

TREKKING STYLE Backpacking along a
well-defined trail with campsites en route. A good-
sized group consists of 2–4 people. Tour companies
run guided, portered trips, but the environmental
impact created by extra people, luggage and rubbish
is unjustifiable.

PERMITS/RESTRICTIONS One-way traffic on the
trail – you cannot hike back to Wayllabamba from
Machu Picchu. The park levies an entrance fee.
Currently access is limited to organized groups.
Check with tourist information in Cuzco or contact
the club listed below.

MAPS Editorial Lima produce a 1:50,000 map of the
trail available from map websites.

INFORMATION

South American Explorers Club, Republica de
Portugal Street, 13th Block Alfonso Ugate, Lima
(Casilla 3714, Lima 100), Peru; or US office: 126
Indian Creek Road, Ithaca, NY 14850.

Ahead is the stiff climb to Abra Warmiwanusqua, Dead Woman's Pass, which is considered the most gruelling part of the trail. At 4200m (13,780ft), the altitude begins to take its toll, but the view back towards the snowy summit of Nevado Wayanay is magnificent. From the pass, steps swoop down between jagged ridges to Paqamayo where the trail crosses the river to another campsite before climbing again to Runkurakay, the Egg Fort. The spectacular views from this neat oval ruin, back to the pass and down the valley of the Paqamayo, would certainly qualify it as a lookout post, but it may once have been a *tambo* (rest-house).

Beyond, the trail skirts marshy lakes and crosses a lower crest before reaching the head of the second pass, Abra Runkurakay (3924m; 12,800ft), from where the snows of the Cordillera Vilcabamba can be seen in the distance on a clear day. By now, the steep inclines and rugged country have made it clear why the Inca's mountain empire never developed wheels.

More steps and a short tunnel gradually lead down past a larger marshy lake dammed by a pile of huge boulders through which the outflow imperceptibly finds its way. An easy traverse suddenly reveals Sayaqmarka, the Fortified Town, perched airily on a sharp spur ahead.

The trail hairpins down sharply to a small campsite by a stream near the restored *tambo* of Qochamarka. On the bend, a flight of steep stone steps leads up to the ruins of Sayaqmarka, whose centrepiece is an outcrop of natural rock. Overgrown steps leading off into the forest suggest it might once have guarded a crossroads.

ABOVE *The specific location and architectural style of the Sayaqmarka ruins suggest that this was the site of an ancient fortification.*
RIGHT *Trekkers get to grips with the altitude on Abra Warmiwanusqua ('Dead Woman's Pass'), the first on the Inca Trail; in the background is Nevado Wayanay.*
OPPOSITE *Sunrise, and the day begins; trekkers begin to pack away their tents on the ridge above Phuyupatamarka, with its sheer drop beyond.*

There's another campsite not far beyond Qochamarka, and then the trail rolls over low spurs before traversing the length of a steep-sided valley. After crossing the marshy remains of a dried-up lake by an Inca causeway, steps lead into a long tunnel the Incas cut into the rock. The cloud forest begins to flower and becomes more luxuriant. Gnarled trees swathed in mosses and lichen support bromeliads, ferns and delicate orchids, often smothered by hummingbirds and butterflies. The trail itself is terraced into the valley side. Be careful here: what looks like a grassy mound beside the track may only be a network of mosses over an abyss.

Just over the last pass, slipping over a ridge at 3580m (11,750ft), there is a poor campsite overlooking Phuyupatamarka, the Town in the Clouds. The stonework of these ruins includes ritual baths and a chamber built into the terracing. In the distance the clearings in the forest that are Intipata and Winaywayna can be seen 1000m (3280ft) below.

From here, the old route traverses the mountain but has fallen into disuse with the discovery of cleverly constructed flights of Inca steps, which plunge a short distance through the forest. There's another short tunnel before the trail descends past a pylon towards the red-roofed *hostal* with its food hall, bar and showers, which is the last place to camp before Machu Picchu. Just 10 minutes away is Winaywayna's ingeniously irrigated concave terracing, ritual baths and restored buildings. The name, said to mean 'forever young', comes from a beautiful orchid growing thereabouts – and there's an undeniable atmosphere of peace and harmony. Intipata lies further up to the west, featuring convex terracing and less restoration. Scrambling up the overgrown terraces will reveal ruins that are half demolished, half held together by the vegetation.

It is possible to reach the lower entrance of Winaywayna by a new modern trail from Km 107 on the Urubamba far below, but this adds to pressure on accommodation, and is not recommended.

The *hostal* is about two hours from Intipunku, the Gate of the Sun. The trail rises and falls through steaming cloud forest until steep steps lead up to a narrow Inca gateway – which turns out not to be Intipunku – that lies just beyond. You should reach the Gate just as the sun rises. On a clear day the spot offers a superb view of Machu Picchu, one that will leave you in awe and convinced that every step to get you here was worth it.

The sheer size of the ruined buildings and extent of the ancient city is amazing. Entering means checking in packs at the lower entrance, but then there's the freedom to roam the ruins, or climb up to the pointed peak of Wayna Picchu to visit its Temple of the Moon, unencumbered by the masses of tourists and daytrippers that descend around lunchtime.

Only remember to leave enough time for catching the train back to Cuzco.

ABOVE *After climbing a steep series of stairs to the Gate of the Sun – Intipunku – trekkers gain their first awe-inspiring sight of the Inca city, Machu Picchu.*
OPPOSITE *A view over Machu Picchu; behind, the Temple of the Moon clings almost impossibly to the slopes of Mt Wayna (also spelled Huayna) Picchu.*

KAÇKAR OF THE PONTIC ALPS

Across serrated ridges, around dark lakes

Black Sea, northeastern Turkey
KATE CLOW

The Pontic Alps, a glaciated granite mountain range in northern Turkey, hugs the coast of the Black Sea. The Alps sweep down as a narrow ribbon from the Russian border in the northeast, bordered on the south by the Coruh River. To the west, trade routes over the Zigana and Kop passes link the medieval entrepot of Erzurum – gateway to Persia (Iran) and last defence against Russia – with the ancient Greek colony of Trabzon on the Black Sea. Northern mountain slopes are wooded, with rhododendrons and pines succeeded at lower levels by chestnut and beech, then by tea plantations and hazelnut groves spilling down towards the waves. In contrast, the dry southern slopes are patched with stone-walled fields and summer pastures where black bulls graze.

The wealth of lakes, streams and springs, variety of afforestation (up to 2100m; 6900ft) and mix of climate mean that these spectacular mountains support an exuberance of spring and summer flowers. The wildlife, which includes bear, wolf and chamois, is far more secretive, although eagles, vultures, Caspian snow cocks, partridges, and many smaller birds haunt the crags.

Once densely inhabited and highly productive, the valleys now ring to the sound of summer returnees from Istanbul or Germany for three short months. The women's clothing, a brilliant contrast to the dour *chador* of Erzurum, is multilayered and brilliantly colourful. In terms of religious influences, devout Christian worship has been replaced (within living memory) by devout Muslim observance, including temperance – rumours abound of residual Greek Orthodox Armenian communities. A scattering of abandoned or converted churches, some dating from the heyday of the Georgian kingdom in the 10th and 11th centuries, recall past glories. The annual Kafkasör festival at Artvin, celebrated with bullfighting and folk dancing, demonstrates the non-Turkish ethnic origins of the inhabitants.

The Kaçkar mountains, forming the northern portion of the Anatolian range in northeastern Turkey, have been inhabited since prehistoric times. In the fourth century BC, Xenophon brought his army of 10,000 Greek mercenary

soldiers back from Persia. After fighting his way across Kurdish territory in a bitter, snowy winter, he crossed the Pontic Alps via the Zigana Pass:

'When the men in front reached the summit and caught sight of the sea there was a great shouting. Xenophon and the rearguard heard it and thought that there were some more enemies attacking in front ... So they rode forward to give support and heard the soldiers shouting out, "The sea! The sea!" and passing the word down the column. When they all got to the top, the soldiers, with tears in their eyes, embraced each other and their generals and captains.'

— *Xenophon, The Persian Expedition*

In 1890, the British explorer Isabella Bird was delighted by the snow: 'Villages of chalets with irregular balconies and steep roofs are perched on the rocky heights or nestle among walnuts, with a blue background of pines above which tower spires and peaks of unsullied snow; ridges rise into fantastic forms and mimicries of minarets and castles; pines, filling gigantic ravines with their blue gloom, stand sentinel over torrents silenced for the winter ... an uplifted snow world of ceaseless surprises under a blue sky full of light, make one fancy oneself in Switzerland, 'til a long train of decorated camels or a turbaned party of armed travellers dissipates the dream.'

— *Journeys in Persia and Kurdistan*

The Kaçkar mountains were discovered as a climbing paradise in the 1980s; and the first commonly available map was drawn in 1988. There are two times of year to trek in these Turkish Alps – high summer, when the snow has

OPPOSITE INSET *These children are from a tiny school in Yaylalar – the only one that remains open. Metin, their schoolteacher, doubles as a guide in summer.*
OPPOSITE *The grassy hollow around Buyuk Deniz and the smaller nearby lake provide an extensive campsite, conveniently placed for the Naletleme Pass.*

TOP *A Kaçkar village is surrounded by a pattern of old stone walls, no longer maintained. Corrugated iron has replaced tiles on the roofs of the inhabited houses.*
ABOVE RIGHT *Wrestlers at the Kafkasör festival pit their strength against one another; children as young as 10 years compete in their own weight classes.*

LOCATION Kaçkar mountain range, Pontic Alps, northern Turkey.

ACCESS Long-distance buses or Turkish Airlines flights from Istanbul to Erzurum or Trabzon. Local buses run Trabzon-Artvin-Yusufeli or Erzurum-Tortum-Yusufeli. Taxi or minibus for 52km (30 miles) of dirt road from Yusufeli to Yaylalar. Supplies available in Yaylalar, Yukari Kavron and Barhal.

START A *pension* at the entrance to Yaylalar village.

FINISH Barhal village.

BEST TIME TO GO Clear skies and firm snow are guaranteed between 15 February and 15 March (winter); in July to September (summer) routefinding is easy.

TREKKING STYLE Jagged granite mountains, partly glaciated, with both glacial and stream-cut valleys. The route runs mainly above the tree line (about 2100m; 6900ft) in rocky valleys and over steep passes, with some scree, especially at altitude. Clear paths at lower levels; cairns at higher levels. A guide is required in winter as cairns/paths are not visible and maps show insufficient detail; self-guided trek or arranged expedition in summer – guides can arrange pack mules (one mule to 3–4 trekkers).

DURATION 10–14 days, depending on weather and optional climbs of Kaçkar and the Altıparmak ridge; about 130km (80 miles) excluding optional summits.

MAX. ALTITUDE Highest pass – unnamed (3305m; 10,845ft); Mount Kaçkar (3932m; 12,900ft).

EQUIPMENT

WINTER – full winter gear including boots, thermals, jacket, vest and gaiters, snow goggles, ice-axe, crampons; lightweight tent and four-season sleeping bag; high-altitude cooker and food.

SUMMER – hiking boots, good wet-weather gear, four-season sleeping bag. Sunscreen, sun hat, water bottle. Daypacks useful for day-trips.

MAPS Download from website: www.kackar-mountains.com

DANGERS Watch out for aggressive sheep-dogs and black bulls.

PERMITS/RESTRICTIONS No permit required.

INFORMATION

Websites:

www.kackarmountains.com (access, accommodation, guides, maps)

www.tempotour.com/kackar.htm

www.gorp.com/gorp/location/asia/turkey

melted from all but the most sheltered valleys, and late winter, when avalanche risk is over, the snow is crusted and the days are lengthening and cloudless. Undoubtedly the summits are most impressive under snow, but all commercial group treks are made in summer.

The two-part trek featured here weaves along the six-fingered ridges of the Altıparmak, and the Kaçkar mountains – and circles Mount Kaçkar, at 3932m (12,900ft) the fifth highest peak in Turkey. The ascent of Kaçkar, using the southern, nontechnical route, is the highlight of the trek, which starts at a rambling *pension* overhanging the dirt road at the entrance to Yaylalar village (still known to the locals as Hevek), a stone and timber settlement on the south bank of the Hevek River. The route rises into the Hevek valley and skirts its cliffs at the western end. From the Hevek Pass, the Anatolian plateau is visible, spread like a dusty blanket checked with lines of poplars, and stretching to Erzurum. The day ends at a tiny rock-encircled lake, Damla Gölü, where the

hardy can bathe in sun-warmed snowmelt. First dawn the following morning is exhilarating. An easy dewy descent through long grasses and flowers into the wide Davali valley ends at a meadow campsite for day two above a primitive *yayla*, or 'summer pasture', where robust black cattle graze.

Forking right for Kavran Pass the following day (three), the route veers, aiming straight at the summit massif of Kaçkar, to dodge between spurs to a narrow nameless pass opening onto the northern side of the range. Views of the serrated edges of the summit sawing into the sky make the heart stop.

ABOVE *Like most of the major peaks, Mount Kaçkar has a cairn with a summit register; every spring local guides erect a new Turkish flag at the summit.*
OPPOSITE *The black bulls are no longer allowed to roam free, but the cream- or ginger-coloured cows can damage tents as they scavenge for food at campsites.*

Below, rocky spikes and spurs obscure the northern trailhead village of Yukarı Kavron. First comes a steep descent to grassy Derebaşı Lake, and an easy contour to Öküz Çayırı Lake – the base camp for technical climbs via the northern glacier of Mount Kaçkar.

A clear path leads steeply to a gaggle of low houses at a junction of two valleys. Yukarı Kavron is a homely, stone village where seasonally bustling cafes, a *pension* and village shop cater for climbers and trekkers. Vast meals of local delicacies such as skewered kebabs, pancakes, fresh yoghurt and halva (*helve*) replenish tired trekkers. When mist shrouds the valley, the villagers light bonfires to guide benighted walkers in.

A lake, Büyük Deniz (*deniz* literally translated is 'sea'), marks day four's campsite, but it is only three hours away up the Çaymakur valley. This is Turkey's deepest high-level lake, set in a basin scooped out of flaking rock and fed by glaciers. Nearby are tiny Metenek Lake and Kara Deniz, all swimmable and with campsites. From here a good path leads upward to shady Naletleme pass, topped all year by snowfields, and onwards to a large campsite at Düpedüzü, in the beautiful valley of the same name.

An almost trackless short cut crosses a dividing ridge to Dilberdüzü, the southern campsite used by groups as a base for nontechnical climbs of Mount Kaçkar (3932m; 12,900ft). For individual trekkers, there is room for a tent or two at Deniz Lake on day five, hidden by scree slopes two hours above, and from here, the summit is four hours away. Climbers circle the lake and climb a snowy valley to pass below the glacier that lies ahead. A climb first over slabs, then scree, leads to the ridge, and a final stiff hour over broken rock ends at the summit, where a cairn and double box hold the summit register. In clear weather, the views are magnificent; the panorama extends from the northern glacier anticlockwise to the dusty lake at Öküz Çayırı, the ridge and Verçenik Peak to the west, and your start point, Deniz Lake below. Two tiny lakes atop the Devil's Rocks lie beneath you, and beyond them the Hevek valley. The descent is by the same route, and, after a night in camp, the return to Yaylalar only takes three to four hours (day six).

The second part of the trek, starting on day seven, leads north from Yaylalar to the Altıparmak massif (still a part of the Kaçkar range). A delightful mule path leads from an arched stone bridge up a side valley to Karamolla, a permanent village of massive houses with only four winter inhabitants. Next is the *yayla* of Körahmet ('blind Ahmet'), named after an outlaw who took refuge here. Beyond the scattered thorns and birches where partridge feed, the path mounts the right bank to climb to a pass leading to Öküz Lake, at the start of

the Altıparmak range. Past Bulut (meaning 'cloud') *yayla*, into Bülbül ('nightingale') valley, the route aims across the valley to a detached spur, Nebisgatur hill, a lovely point from which to view the range. On the far side of this is Kara Lake – *kara* translates as 'black'. Set in a stony valley above rattling waterfalls, it is the base camp for climbs on Altıparmak Ridge. Serrated ridges ahead invite exploration; there are several routes onward, mostly suitable for day climbs, and rewarded by glimpses of the north side of the range – green and lush below the misty blanket.

After completing your day-trip excursions, the final walk down to the village of Barhal from Kara Lake goes past pretty *yaylas* with watermills and beehives, blooming meadows and apple orchards, then descends into forest on the left bank of the Barhal River. Above the town, nestling in trees next to the school, is the beautiful Georgian 10th-century basilica – the Church of the Four Apostles, the sharp roof echoing the ridges around. Converted to a mosque 40 years ago, the simple, dressed-stone exterior is decorated with crosses reminiscent of ancient tombstones, which share with the mountains the term *kaçkars*. Look inside at the power of the main piers – set off by carvings of tiny angels – supporting the stone roof. The frescoes survived a thousand years of worship to succumb to a thoughtless coat of whitewash. Arch shapes and stone motifs were later inherited by the conquering Selçuk Turks.

The Pontic Alps always were a wild refuge for the weak struggling against the powerful rulers of the world, representing individuality versus conformity. As the sparkling valley leads downhill to the plains, the Kaçkar, behind, lift up their heads to the light and shade of the sky.

ABOVE *The ridge of the 10th-century church roof at Barhal echoes the shape of the skyline around. Master masons from here were in great demand in Istanbul.*
RIGHT *The Altıparmak range, less heavily grazed than the north side of the range, has a huge profusion of wild flowers, including water-loving primulas.*
OPPOSITE *The awesome scale of a glacier on the north of Mount Kaçkar; the scoured rock is evidence of the grinding power of this gritty ice.*

LUKPE LA

Crossing the glacier gateway

Karakorum mountain range, Pakistan
STEVE RAZZETTI

At 5700m (18,700ft), the Lukpe La (*la* is a 'pass') is the highpoint of this seldom undertaken but utterly exhilarating traverse of the northern Karakorum. From the village of Passu on the Karakorum Highway in Hunza to Askole in Baltistan, this route is one of the most strenuous treks in Pakistan.

The journey across 260km (160 miles) of spectacularly remote and difficult country will take a fit party three weeks. Few places on the planet today are as inaccessible as these peaks and valleys, and those who would venture here should be aware that, in an emergency, help is a very long way away. All members should be well versed in the techniques of roped glacier travel, crevasse rescue and mountain navigation.

Geographically, this trek is unique in that it is the only way one can legally cross the Karakorum watershed, part of the great Central Asiatic Divide. Standing on the vast windswept *pamirs* (grazing grounds) of the Shimshal Pass (4460m; 14,630ft) you look ahead into valleys that drain their waters into the boundless shimmering salt flats of the Takli Makan Desert. Behind you, the fearsome gorges carrying the headwaters of the Shimshal River (a section northeast of Shimshal village known as the Pamir-i-Tang) eventually debouch their silt-laden torrents into the Indus. Here, waters that rise within a kilometre of each other are destined to incredibly different fates – either to evaporate under the furnace-like heat of a desert sun, or languidly travel thousands of kilometres to the Arabian Sea.

Much of the country traversed lies within areas nominally designated as the Khunjerab and Central Karakorum national parks in Pakistan. Founded in

1975 and 1994 respectively, with the primary intention of protecting rapidly shrinking populations of Marco Polo sheep, snow leopard and brown bear, the administration of these important reserves has always been controversial.

What is beyond doubt, however, is that within their bounds lie some of the most beautiful and rugged tracts of mountainous country on earth. From idyllic orchards, patchwork farmland and the tranquil calm of Ishmaili villages in Hunza – dwarfed by snowpeaks and presenting what British mountaineer Eric Shipton described as 'the ultimate manifestation of mountain grandeur' – this route follows the Shimshal River east to its headwaters below Shimshal Pass, just a few kilometres from the border with China's Xinjang Province. Then it swings south up the Braldu valley to the Lukpe La, Snow Lake (or Lukpe Lawo) and the legendary mountains that surround it.

Beyond apocryphal accounts of skirmishes between Hunzakut and Balti tribesmen in the area – before advancing glaciation made such adventurism impossible – little is known about the ancient history of man's incursions here. The people of Hunza and Baltistan have virtually no written record, having long relied on elaborate oral traditions of storytelling. They also share a level of superstition and a propensity for exaggeration that nicely blur the concept of historical truth.

The first European to cross the Shimshal Pass from the north in 1889 was one of Britain's great imperial adventurers, Francis Younghusband. He had his eye on the Pamir mountains to the northwest, however, and after a brief look into the top of the Pamir-i-Tang he re-crossed the pass and continued his explorations in what is today Chinese Turkestan.

Three years later it was another British officer, Colonel Cockerill, who finally penetrated these awesome defiles. The opening decades of the 20th century saw further sporadic exploration by the likes of Kenneth Mason and RCF Schomberg. However, it was the members of Eric Shipton's seminal 1937 expedition who finally unravelled the complex geographic mysteries that had for so long shrouded the central Karakorum. Finally, the 'blank on the map' was filled in.

OPPOSITE INSET *Not for the faint-hearted! Crossing the second* jhola *at Ziarat on the walk to Shimshal. High water in summer may preclude this exciting shortcut.*
OPPOSITE *Pausing to rest on the descent south from the Lukpe La into the Sim Gang basin. The spectacular peak appearing from the cloud is Braldu Brakk (6200m; 20,340ft), first climbed in 1956 by Durbin and Williams.*
TOP *The Sim Gang basin, viewed in its entirety from the Hispar La.*
ABOVE RIGHT *Shimshal village, a respite from the severity of the surrounding country, had not heard the sound of a motor vehicle until recently, when a road was built here.*
PAGES 66–67 *An elderly Bhutanese in contemplation at the ruins of Drukgyel Dzong, a fortified monastery built in 1650, situated in the Paro River valley.*

the old route: reaching the village used to take two long days, which involved traversing unstable scree at river level, crossing dizzying *jholas* (wire bridges) and negotiating the Malangutti glacier (from the centre of this iceflow the snowplastered north face of Disteghil Sar is spectacularly revealed).

Shuwert, the summer grazing settlement on the Shimshal Pass, is three gruelling days from the village. The trail initially heads north into the desolate valley of Zardgar Bin, but soon climbs away east up steep screes to the Shashmirk La (4160m; 13,650ft), from which the true majesty of the country is revealed. South, across the Shimshal valley, the white ice of Yazghil glacier carves away through barren ranges to the vast mountain wall that forms the Hispar-Shimshal watershed. Disteghil Sar (7885m; 25,870ft), Kunyang Chhish (7852m; 25,760ft), Pumari Chhish (7350m; 24,115ft) and Kanjut Sar (7760m; 25,460ft) are all visible among a snowy sea of lesser summits. Northeast, the fantastic eroded flanks and ancient river terraces of the Pamir-i-Tang stretch away into the distance.

Two brutal days of constant ascent and descent on hideously steep and loose trails then take you to the pastures at Shujerab, where the gorges finally give way to fine open country and the Shimshal Pass.

A few days' rest here, among the women and children who spend their summers tending huge flocks of sheep, goats and yaks, will both entertain and acclimatize you. The lakes which crown the pass are a stopover for many species of migrating ducks and wading birds, and the nearby plains of Zhit Bhadav provide a backdrop of epic proportions. Your Shimshali hosts will arrange yaks to accompany you into the Braldu valley; they carry both men and kit across the river. The possibilities for exploratory hikes and climbs in this area are almost endless, but most travellers will be anxious to press on to the crux of the trek. Once you are across the Braldu River and your yaks have gone back, you are committed to crossing the Lukpe La. Serious stuff.

The necessity of using Shimshali yaks to cross the Braldu River obliges travellers to start their journey from Passu. The domain of the Shimshalis effectively begins immediately across the Hunza River from the village of Passu, where Shimshali men insist on doing any portering into their territory. This may seem headstrong, but it should not be ignored that many are excellent mountaineers and high-altitude porters.

Shimshal village itself is a skilfully tended and verdant oasis of whitewashed houses, poplar trees and apricot orchards. The surrounding fields and grazing livestock support a population of over 1000 people – a community which retains a degree of self-sufficiency that is rare today. The building of a road into the formidable Shimshal valley has begun, bypassing most of the difficulties on

ABOVE *The Shimshalis drive all their livestock through the awesome defile of the Pamir-i-Tang on their annual migration to the remote settlement of Shuwert.*
RIGHT *Mother and child basking in Shuwert's summer sun; several hundred Shimshalis tend their flocks here, sending butter, cheese and curds back to Shimshal.*

ABOVE *The rock spires of the west Biafo wall, described by Fanny Bullock Workman as the 'Valhalla' of Biafo.*

LOCATION Northern and central Karakorum ranges, Pakistan.

WHEN TO GO July–August offer the best chance of stable, fine weather. Crevasses open up as summer progresses.

START Passu village, on the Karakorum Highway in Hunza.

FINISH Askole village in Baltistan.

DURATION Approximately 21 days (200km; 125 miles).

MAX. ALTITUDE Lukpe La (5700m; 18,700ft).

TECHNICAL CONSIDERATIONS Expertise on prolonged glacier travel is essential.

EQUIPMENT Four-season sleeping bags, tents, food and cooking utensils, and full winter mountaineering equipment (including crampons and ice axe) for both members and porters is essential.

TREKKING STYLE Backpacking with porters.

PERMITS/RESTRICTIONS Advance permit necessary; US$50 is charged per person for one month.

MAPS From US Army Map Service, 1:250,000, series U-502, sheet No. NJ 43–15 (Shimshal).

DANGERS Avalanches are a real threat on Lukpe La. Trekkers need to be able to recognize signs of a crevasse, judge deteriorating snow conditions or a potential avalanche, and understand oncoming bad weather and fronts. Also, come prepared for potential hypothermia with suitably warm wet- and windproof clothing, and learn how to recognize the early signs of this condition.

INFORMATION

Nazir Sabir Expeditions (outfitter for Karakorum range, Pakistan): e-mail: info@nazirsabir.com
Website: www.nazirsabir.com

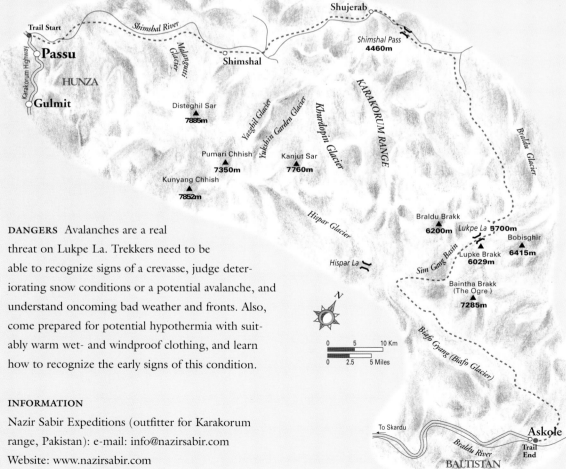

Descending east from the Shimshal Pass you enter a valley that has seen but a handful of foreigners in the last century. Just two days' walk to the north the Braldu flows into the almost mythical Shaksgam – today in Chinese territory, alas – which rises north of Ladakh and drains the northern slopes of the biggest peaks in the Karakorum: K2, Broad Peak and the Gasherbrum group. South, the valley is almost immediately blocked by the rubble-blackened, convoluted and thoroughly appalling snout of the Braldu glacier.

There are no trails or cairns from this point until you leave the snout of the Biafo glacier a couple of hours from Askole, so proficient route-finding is essential. The lower section of the 40km (25-mile) Braldu glacier consists of a labyrinth of ice towers and crevasses. Though the ground above is treacherous and steep, it must be traversed until a safe way onto the smooth tongue of ice – which eventually appears in the centre of the glacier – can be found.

The height of the snow line, as well as number and size of crevasses encountered will vary, often dramatically, from season to season. In such a remote location the consequences of an accident could be fatal, so rope up and tread carefully! Available mapping of the upper Braldu is unreliable, but a safe bet is to follow the eastern edge of the medial moraine until the pass appears ahead. Do not be tempted by any of the enormous tributaries coming in from the west. The main glacier eventually sweeps away up westwards to the pass, which is a very long but gradual ascent.

Few places on earth today are as truly remote, challenging and unbelievably spectacular as the Lukpe La. From the crest, a panorama of stupefying magnificence is revealed. Behind you to the north, the icebound Karakorum diminishes into the lifeless brown ravines and deserts of Turkestan. Ahead, the north face of Baintha Brakk, a.k.a. The Ogre (7285m; 23,900ft), rears above the blinding glare of the Sim Gang basin and Snow Lake – vast névé (firn) fields that were long thought to be a genuine icecap. The apparently smooth surface of the Sim Gang is far from benign however; beneath the snow are complex systems of enormous crevasses. Snow conditions are usually terrible after 9am, so travel early and keep the rope on until you reach the moraines at the head of Biafo glacier.

Distances here are incredibly deceptive. Descending the 35km (22 miles) from Lukpe La to the moraine camp usually referred to as 'Sim Gang base camp' may look straightforward after Braldu, but allow 12–14 hours. Though you are still at least three days from Askole and the road out to Skardu, the Biafo is a friendly glacier by Karakorum standards and you may finally relax and enjoy the superb scenery. Spend a day here spying out routes on the rock towers of the west Biafo wall, and another revelling in the sudden verdure of the alpine meadows at Baintha. Ascend Baintha Peak (5300m; 17,390ft) for one last dose of Karakorum magnificence – this easy summit affords close-up views of the entire Ogre and Latok ranges and is a fitting finale to such an odyssey, before you make your way to Askole village.

LEFT *Looking down the Biafo glacier's frozen super-highway towards Askole – and the approaching finale of a challenging trek. Almost 5km (3 miles) wide on its upper reaches, this gargantuan ice flow is over 1000m (3300ft) deep and moves over 100m (330ft) annually.*

Ladakh, northern India
SEB MANKELOW

Sandwiched between the Karakorum to the north, Tibet to the east, and the Himalaya to the south, India's remote and high-altitude desert region of Ladakh endures ferociously cold winters. In early January, consistently low temperatures eventually coerce the region's Zanskar River into winter dormancy. The swift currents and boiling rapids are calmed, and slowly they solidify into an icy thoroughfare. The brief annual life of the Zanskar River trek has begun. Walking on the frozen river by day and sleeping in caves and Zanskari houses at night, this winter journey transports trekkers through terrain that for 10 months of the year is only accessible to ibex and those rafting the river in the brief summer.

Draining the Zanskar valley into the mighty Indus, the Zanskar River has carved a serpentine gorge that in places is over 1000m (3300ft) in depth. Trekking along this river course in the depths of winter is a fascinating cultural and geological experience – a fitting reward for a tough and hazardous route to a valley reputed to be one of the coldest inhabited places on Earth. Squashed between the Zanskar range to the north and the Greater Himalaya to the south, the Zanskar valley is remote and largely accessible only on foot. During the brief summer, a single thread of a road – predominantly unsurfaced – links the valley to the rest of the Indian continent. Otherwise, all access is confined to those who trek across the high mountain passes.

In winter these routes are impassable; hampered by heavy snows, the isolated Zanskari communities settle into a traditional way of life that has changed little through generations. Winter holds this ancient kingdom captive for up to seven months of every year, yet, ironically, the bitterly low temperatures do provide Zanskaris with a brief window of escape. Locally referred to as *chaddar*, the frozen rivers effectively act as 'winter roads'. Originally a winter trade route, the Zanskar River is perhaps the greatest of all the *chaddar* journeys. Linking remote Zanskari villages with the Indus valley and the bazaars in Leh (Ladakh's administrative capital), this route was once used to export the prized

commodities of butter and cheese. More recently, it is used as a means to transport children to boarding schools in Leh for the spring term. Inevitably, Western trekkers have also begun to frequent the river, although the extreme cold and arduous nature of the trek deter all but the most determined.

An impressive one-hour flight carries the trekker from Delhi over the Western Himalaya to Leh. While acclimatizing here at 3500m (11,500ft), it may be possible to enjoy one of the several Buddhist festivals scheduled during the winter months. Once acclimatized, there are provisions to buy, and your guide and porters to meet. Undertaking the frozen river trek without an experienced guide is not advisable.

From Leh, a cold – and at times hair-raising – bus journey to the start of the trek at Chilling introduces the trekker to the Zanskar River at its confluence with the Indus. A scatter of dwellings, Chilling is home to Ladakh's most famous smiths. Craftsmen in gold, silver, copper and brass, the villagers are descendants of skilled Nepali workers who in the 16th century were invited by the king of Ladakh to manufacture religious images and objects (it is possible that 'Zanskar' derives from the Tibetan *zangs-dkar*, referring to white copper).

After spending the night at Chilling, trekkers set foot on the river for the first time. It becomes quickly apparent which ice surfaces offer purchase and which do not. Falling over can become a common occurrence, even for Zanskaris, and unless deemed serious a tumble is usually appreciated with hearty laughter! This is, however, a potentially hazardous trek and from the outset it is prudent for trekkers and guide to travel in a group. A surprise dunking is unlikely, but possible. Some sections of ice are deceptively thin and the river always harbours sections of open water that refuse to freeze. Many of these are easily negotiable; others require sure-footed care.

OPPOSITE INSET *A Zanskari porter tows his homemade sledge across thick river ice; the ice is so untainted, pebbles are clearly visible on the riverbed below.*
OPPOSITE *Leaving Zanskar, red-clad trekkers on the river between Hanamil and Tserac Do are dwarfed by the impressive strata of geological folds (a syncline).*

TOP *Zanskari porters circumvent an open-water section of the frozen river; although precarious, negotiating the ice ledge is preferable to wading.*
ABOVE RIGHT *At the end of day two, trekkers and Zanskari porters share the warmth of driftwood fires in the soot-blackened cave, Dip Yogma.*

Nevertheless, the unique experience of travelling on river-ice is something to savour. The trekker is enticed by the remarkable scenery to continue around every twist and turn. Several hours from Chilling a rust-red mountain dominates the route ahead and from this point the gorge begins to deepen and the landscape to intensify. If ice conditions are favourable, the first night on the river is often spent at Yogma Shingra, a small rocky shelf and beach beneath a conglomerate cliff. Huddled around a driftwood fire, the silence that descends on the gorge is punctuated by sharp cracks and groans as river-ice shifts in the falling temperatures.

The next three days follow a similar routine. An early start effectively combats the insidious cold and maximizes the chance of reaching the preferred caves by nightfall. The gorge continues to grow in stature as the route weaves back and forth, unfolding around each river bend. In places where the river-ice is thin or nonexistent, the trekker has little choice but to scale the rocky sides and undertake unprotected traverses above open water. If the rock is steep and featureless, and the water not too deep, then a quick wade may suffice. Failing that, a deviation to several hundred feet above the river, on easier ground, may offer a strenuous alternative to an otherwise lengthy wait for the river to refreeze.

Indeed, fluctuations in temperature constantly modify ice conditions. Sweeping corrugated surfaces track the demise and eventual solidification of river currents, and occasionally the ice is so transparent that boulders are visible on the riverbed below. Temperature also influences the trekking day and breaks usually coincide with a welcome pocket of sunshine. Tucked out of the wind it is often warm enough to enjoy a cup of tea and air damp boots and other equipment. Transition from sun to shade is marked by dramatic variations in temperature. Deep in the gorge the route persistently moves between these two extremes, making the correct selection of clothing layers particularly challenging. The second day ends far from the sun's warmth at Dip Yogma, a large cave well above the river. The ash floor and soot-blackened roof bear testament to the generations of Zanskaris that have sought shelter here.

Leaving Dip Yogma on the third day, the route negotiates several areas notorious for poor ice formation and, depending on the severity of conditions, trekkers can spend the night at Nerac or several hours further upriver near the tributary that leads to the village of Lingshet.

Nerac consists of a handful of houses perched high above the river. A steep climb at dusk to the barren fields that surround this village offers a wonderful expanse of star-studded sky. Nerac marks the climatic transition from the Ladakh rain shadow to the true Himalayan winter; from here on, snow cover steadily increases. The precipitous gorge also undergoes a transition and by the end of the fourth day of trekking, the landscape becomes more open. Again, there is a choice of locations in which to overnight and if poor conditions have again hampered progress, then Tserac Do, a small cave perched on a rocky outcrop, is a comfortable but sometimes breezy option. For those making

ABOVE *Across the river from Hanamil, a wind-sculpted tower of conglomerate marks one of many trails leading away from the frozen river towards Zangla.*

OPPOSITE *On day three, a trekker and her Zanskari guide cross a narrow shelf to avoid the soft water-soaked ice just inches away from her boots.*

good time, there are several smaller caves and overhanging rocks further up-river; your guide should know whether these can be reached before nightfall.

After several hours of walking on day five, the trekker arrives in Sham, or Lower Zanskar. Upon nearing the small village of Hanamil, there are opportunities to leave the river and follow a combination of the snow-packed trails that link Zanskar's villages in winter. The severity of the gorge is long gone and the river now cuts along a vast U-shaped valley that has been hewn by the immense glaciers that once crept northwards from the Greater Himalaya. It is now possible to travel to Padum on either bank of the Zanskar River and the overnight villages change accordingly. Travelling on the eastern side of the river, the fifth night of the trek can be spent in the village of Zangla.

On easier terrain, the following day's walk to Stongde offers the first views of the 6500m (21,000ft) peaks of the Greater Himalaya. After a further half-day, the trekker arrives at the foot of these mountains and the village of Padum, lying at 3600m (11,900ft).

Having travelled with a Zanskari guide and porters, the trekker has had the privilege of participating in what is essentially a traditional winter journey. On arriving in Zanskar, there are further opportunities to participate in Zanskari winter life by staying in a local home, and meeting the families of the guide and porters. This is a rich and rewarding experience. After sampling mutton *sku* and the alcoholic *chang*, all that remains is to retrace the *chaddar* to Chilling on the return trip to Leh.

ABOVE *Leaving the steeper sections of the gorge behind, Zanskari porters head towards Hanamil, the first permanent habitation in Sham, or lower Zanskar.*

OPPOSITE *As temperatures on the river rise and fall, massive forces of expansion and contraction buckle and fracture the river-ice, creating unique sculptures.*

LOCATION Zanskar River, Ladakh, northern India.

WHEN TO GO The most reliable period for the formation of river-ice is early January to mid-February, although conditions will inevitably vary from year to year. Completion of the trek is dependent upon good river-ice conditions.

START/FINISH A round trip starting at the current roadhead at Chilling (approx. 5 hours from Leh by bus); trekkers usually walk in and out of Zanskar via the same route.

DURATION 14 days (260km; 160 miles). Poor river-ice conditions may increase the duration. Shorter variations of the trek are possible by simply retracing the route before reaching Padum. The Lingshet trek is a popular 4-day (8-day round trip) option.

MAX. ALTITUDE Sometimes, detours up to passes in the gorge – rising to 4000m (13,000ft) – and down again to the river are necessary.

TECHNICAL CONSIDERATIONS Serious expedition. Trekkers must be fit and well versed in living in extreme cold. They must also be prepared to wade through open water and undertake exposed rock climbing and scrambling, all in subzero temperatures. Usual daytime temperatures in the shade range from -5° to -25°C (23° to -13°F).

EQUIPMENT Suitable thermal clothing, boots and sleeping gear to cope with extreme weather and temperatures as low as -40°C (-40°F). Trekking poles, rope, a towel and spare boots for wading may be useful. All consumables (food, stove and fuel, cooking utensils) for the outward and return journey must be purchased in Leh prior to departure as there is no guarantee that these goods will be available in Zanskar.

TREKKING STYLE Ice trekking with a local guide, cook and porters. Trekkers overnight in caves and Zanskari houses. Itinerary and day-length are subject to local river-ice conditions. It is not advisable to undertake the trek without an experienced guide.

MAPS A 1:350,000 map of the area is published by Éditions Olizane, Genève.

PERMITS/RESTRICTIONS Currently none, although it is advisable to check the political situation in Zanskar and neighbouring areas.

INFORMATION

Websites:

www.jktourism.org (Jammu & Kashmir tourism)

www.ibexpeditions.com

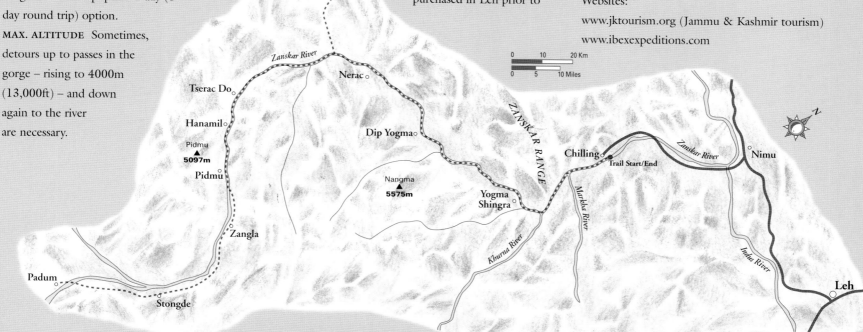

A TIGER'S LAIR
& A SACRED PEAK

Land of the Thunder Dragon

Bhutan, eastern Himalaya

JUDY ARMSTRONG

Bhutan is a jealously guarded kingdom in the bosom of the Himalaya. The Bhutanese call it Shangri-la and guard its isolation as fiercely as the snow leopard – elusive among the sacred peaks – guards its lair. Squashed between the giants of India and Tibet, Bhutan has for centuries served as a buffer against conflict. While its borders have been shaped by religion and geography, its soul has remained intact. Bhutan remains a Buddhist stronghold, and maintains a hereditary monarchy.

But as this tiny kingdom enters the new millennium, it teeters on the cusp of change. King Jigme Singye Wangchuck, an educated and well-regarded man, recently denationalized the tourism industry. This means that the only restriction on tourists entering the country is now based on cost; the old figure of 3000 entry permits per year is no longer enforceable.

The nation is rife with anomalies. Roads were built in the 1960s but hill-farmers walk up to five days to reach them. Television was introduced in 1999, but most houses don't have toilets. Astrologers are consulted before doctors, education comes second to hand-harvesting the rice crop.

All Bhutanese wear the traditional outfit: *kira* for women (a floor-length dress made from a brightly coloured rectangle of cloth) and *gho* for men (a long robe hoisted to knee-length and worn with a tight belt), but in the temples, monks wear T-shirts under their crimson robes.

Shops in the town of Paro often have no doors so women, with babies on their backs, climb over ladder-stiles through glassless windows for their shopping. Purchases could be dried yak meat, Nike trainers, bamboo rice strainers or glossy imported lipstick.

The landscape is enormous, yet delicate: Bhutan is on the latitude of Cairo, yet almost a quarter of its area is under permanent snow; jagged, snow-crowned peaks soar behind patchwork fields crammed with crops of rice and potatoes. Churning, glacier-fed rivers become irrigation trickles, broad-hipped monasteries shade tiny temples. Forests of golden larch support strands of lacy

lichen; crested hoopoes hop in the shadow of eagles. Bhutanese culture is founded firmly on Bhuddist philosophy and beliefs. The most obvious incarnations are the great white *dzongs*, or fortified monasteries, which guard valleys and towns. Some, such as the Paro and Punakha *dzongs*, are richly decorated with gold and scarlet; others are more subdued. Equally prominent are the *chortens*. These small structures contain religious artefacts and prayer wheels which are spun so that the blessings inside may be released. They are found on walking tracks, near rivers and mountain passes. Here, too, are prayer flags, long strips of red, white, blue, yellow and green which flap and snap in the wind, sending off with the breeze blessings for luck, and for the deceased.

While many tourists target Bhutan for its festivals and way of life, it is also a haven for trekkers. To minimize the impact on the environment, there is a restriction on numbers of walkers on the trekking routes and every party must engage a guide. Littering is not permitted, and no infrastructure exists apart from designated campsites.

Treks can last for two or three days in the lowlands, and up to 23 days for the high-altitude Snowman trek.

The route described here covers the middle ground: a hike up to the campsite of Jangothang (lying at 4090m; 13,420ft), returning the same way or via a different valley. It visits remote valleys to give a glimpse of the sacred peak Chomolhari, but stops short of an altitude where health problems are likely to occur. All peaks are sacred to the Bhutanese – and as a result, serious mountaineering is banned, but Chomolhari, the most sacred of all, is special. The name translates as 'goddess of the mountain'. It is Bhutan's third highest at 7314m (23,997ft).

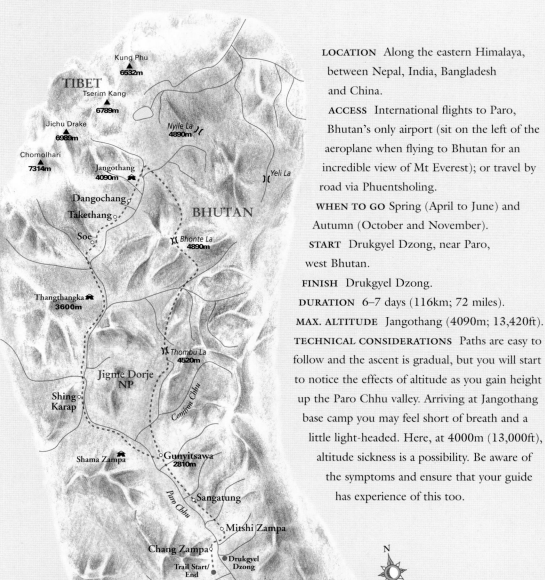

LOCATION Along the eastern Himalaya, between Nepal, India, Bangladesh and China.

ACCESS International flights to Paro, Bhutan's only airport (sit on the left of the aeroplane when flying to Bhutan for an incredible view of Mt Everest); or travel by road via Phuentsholing.

WHEN TO GO Spring (April to June) and Autumn (October and November).

START Drukgyel Dzong, near Paro, west Bhutan.

FINISH Drukgyel Dzong.

DURATION 6–7 days (116km; 72 miles).

MAX. ALTITUDE Jangothang (4090m; 13,420ft).

TECHNICAL CONSIDERATIONS Paths are easy to follow and the ascent is gradual, but you will start to notice the effects of altitude as you gain height up the Paro Chhu valley. Arriving at Jangothang base camp you may feel short of breath and a little light-headed. Here, at 4000m (13,000ft), altitude sickness is a possibility. Be aware of the symptoms and ensure that your guide has experience of this too.

EQUIPMENT Walking boots, small backpack (everything else will be carried on the pack horses), layered clothing to cope with extremes of temperature (it can be hot during the day, and freezing at night at higher elevations).
Water filters or sterilization tablets are a good addition to boiling river water.

TREKKING STYLE Pleasant hiking on good trails through wild and beautiful terrain. You must trek with a guide and a trek support team of horseman, cook and at least one helper; make the most of it by interacting with them and the local people you meet along the way. Camping equipment supplied may be basic – take your own sleeping bag and mat.

PERMITS/RESTRICTIONS Tourists need a visa to enter Bhutan, and must pre-arrange their itineraries through recognized tour operators. An all-inclusive daily rate is charged; this covers transport within the country, food, accommodation, guide, trek support team, and so on. The rate, quoted in US dollars, may seem high but it offers good value for money, providing access to a unique country and culture.

INFORMATION
Websites: www.bhutantrekking.co.uk
www.classic.mountainzone.com/hike/bhutan
www.himalayankingdoms.com
www.bhutan-info.org

The best trekking option is to start with a day-hike from Paro valley to the Tiger's Lair monastery – called Taktsang by the Bhutanese. (Taktsang Goemba, or 'monastery', is a more accurate name as it actually comprises several building complexes. Taktsang Lhakhang ('temple') is sometimes used too – though this Bhutanese word also describes the main shrine within each temple – so the *goemba* contains many *lhakhangs*.)

It is a four-hour walk, ascending 1000m (3300ft) to reach a level of 3100m (10,200ft) – useful acclimatization for the trek to follow. The track climbs past ricefields, through juniper and pine forests, past prayer flags, and *chortens* (these should be passed in a clockwise direction).

The best view of Tiger's Lair is from a rocky ledge that runs parallel to the monastery. A fire destroyed much of this temple in April 1998; rebuilding has begun but the fire was so intense that even the rockface was damaged. The monastery is a jumble of white buildings, impossibly attached to the black cliff. It can be reached using the flying fox cable mechanism across the ravine, but foreigners are not yet permitted to visit until the main rebuilding work is completed as it is presently too dangerous. Looking into the ravine, and at the spindly wires that cross it, you'll be glad not to be making the trip.

The trek up to Jangothang starts the next day, from the ruined fortress at Drukgyel Dzong (2580m; 8410ft). This is where Tibetan armies were finally forced to retreat by the Bhutanese. A dirt track wanders from the *dzong* up the Paro Chhu valley (*chhu* means 'river' or 'water'), following the line of the Paro River's foaming torrent. The valley is fertile and a crazy patchwork of rice paddies covers every inch of land.

At intervals along the track are traditional houses of stone and mud. They are three storeys high: animals live in the lowest layer, people in the middle, and hay or food is dried under the roof. The houses all have white walls and carved wooden, glassless windows intricately painted with auspicious Buddhist symbols. The raised roofs are made of wooden shingles held down with rocks; there are no chimneys so smoke from the open cooking fires makes its way out through whatever crevices it finds. Soon the ricefields give way to crops of oats, chillies and potatoes. Prayer flags by the river flutter in the breeze, and water-powered prayer wheels spin with the current.

After passing the army post at Gunyitsawa (2810m; 9160ft), the campsite for the first night is reached. In a peaceful meadow by the river, the trek team will set up tents, folding chairs and tables before serving dinner under the stars.

For the next two days, the track wanders steadily up the valley, crossing and re-crossing the river on wooden cantilever bridges. Waterfalls stream down the steep valley sides and the trees seem to glow in the clear high-altitude air. On the second day from Drukgyel Dzong the track enters the Jigme Dorje National Park. It is Bhutan's largest protected forest area and home to endangered species including snow leopard, red panda and the hairy-coated takin – which has the appearance of a cross between a gnu and a musk deer. Famous

OPPOSITE *This sturdy stone shelter is the focal point at the Jangothang campsite; fires are built in a central pit on the floor and pack-horse harnesses hang from the walls.*
RIGHT *Making light of the rain … October and November are peak trekking months, and generally dry, but in the mountains the weather can change at any time.*

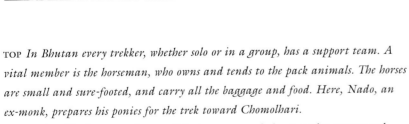

TOP *In Bhutan every trekker, whether solo or in a group, has a support team. A vital member is the horseman, who owns and tends to the pack animals. The horses are small and sure-footed, and carry all the baggage and food. Here, Nado, an ex-monk, prepares his ponies for the trek toward Chomolhari.*

ABOVE *A trekker's tent and a small fortress on a rock droop under unseasonal snow, at the Jangothang campsite. Even in the dry months of October and November, which are the most popular for trekking, snow is a possibility, particularly at this altitude (4090m; 13,420ft).*

ABOVE RIGHT *The sacred peak of Chomolhari glows in the dawn light. Bhutan's third highest summit, rising as it does to a height of 7314m (23,997ft), its name translates as 'goddess of the mountain'.*

biologist George Schaller called it a 'beestung moose' due to its similarity in size to the North American moose – and its humped nose! The wildlife is exotic, with constant sightings of golden birds with long blue tails, cheeky hoopoes with spiky apricot headcrests, and black-and-white butterflies with intricately painted wings.

The second night's camp is at Thangthangka, a meadow at 3600m (11,800ft) with a small stone shelter near a cedar grove. Shortly after leaving here in the morning, Chomolhari reveals herself, then disappears again. Anticipation builds, and as the 4000m (13,000ft) mark is passed, the landscape changes. Huge rock amphitheatres are lined with crashing waterfalls, and glacial debris lies in great lumps on the widening valley floor. This is yak coun-

try. These shaggy beasts are used as pack animals – and for meat. Rich and dark, it's worth four times that of beef. The yak's tail hair is used to make altar brushes. Herds of rare blue sheep (*bharal*) are also likely to be sighted here.

Now houses are few and small, and many have green fodder draped over walls to dry. It is food for the yaks in winter, as even these hardy animals can't fend for themselves when snow lies as high as the second-storey windows. One house is owned by a Tibetan refugee family. The living layer is a single, large room with thick wooden floorboards, and sliding wooden shutters over the glassless windows. A tall dresser serves as an altar; on here, seven small bowls full of holy water are placed before a shrine. Black-and-white pictures of their king are pasted onto the walls, and dried meat and chillies hang from a

wooden beam. Soon after passing this house, Jangothang base camp, at a height of 4090m (13,420ft), and the giant icy pyramid of Chomolhari come into view. This huge mountain rising immediately behind the campsite is surely one of the most wonderful views in the Himalaya.

From here the choices are multiple: trekkers can continue over the 4890m (16,045ft) pass, Nyile La, toward Thimphu or Laya, then turn east over the remote and spectacular Bhonte La or retrace their route along the Paro Chhu (river). In order to complete a six- to seven-day trek, the quickest way back is the two- or three-day hike down the Paro – but if time, budgets and weather allow, these alternative routes offer spectacular sights into more hidden corners of this mountain paradise.

KHARKHIRAA & TURGEN
Between twin peaks

Altai mountain range, western Mongolia
GRAHAM TAYLOR

While many people think of Mongolia as undulating steppe – or desert – the region surrounding these landscapes offers the adventurous trekker a wilderness experience of alpine valleys, glaciated peaks, and herding families with their yaks and camels – but with a Mongolian flavour. There is even the slim chance of seeing a snow leopard.

Lying between China and Siberia, Mongolia is the second largest country in Asia, and with just 2.2 million people (1997 census) has by far the lowest population density. Once part of the former Soviet bloc, Mongolia has maintained independence since 1991 and its government is democratically elected. This country's greatest claim to fame is that it was the birthplace of Genghis Khan, the warrior who during the late 12th and early 13th centuries expanded the Mongol Empire from Poland across the Asian continent to Japan and down to Burma (Myanmar). It is the greatest empire the world has seen.

The twin peaks of Mounts Kharkhiraa and Turgen are located in Uvs Aimag (*aimag* meaning 'province') in the far northwest, home to snow leopard, ibex and argali big-horned sheep. Rising vertically for almost 3500m (11,500ft) from the basin of Lake Uvs, these glaciated peaks form a stunning backdrop to the surrounding desert lowlands. Uvs Province is situated approximately 1500km (900 miles) from Ulaanbaatar (Ulan Bator), Mongolia's capital city. It is a region of remarkable biodiversity and dominated by the depression of Lake Uvs, Mongolia's largest lake in surface area, as well as the Boorog Deliin Els – the world's northernmost desert sand dunes. In the summer months, nomadic herders move their herds of horses, sheep, yaks, and camels into river valleys to graze on alpine pastures. White *gers* (yurts), the dwellings of Mongolia's herdspeople, are a familiar sight here.

The peaks of Turgen and Kharkhiraa lie in the Turgen Strictly Protected Area which belongs to the greater Altai-Sayan biodiversity region, and forms part of the World Wide Fund for Nature's (WWF) project in Mongolia. These mountains are an isolated satellite range of the Mongol Altai Nuruu, which in turn is part of a mountain ring – a belt that stretches from the south Gobi Desert through Kazakhstan to the Tien Shan mountains in northern Pakistan.

The adventurer will find many trekking options in the Turgen Strictly Protected Area, although arguably the finest is a through-trek of 100km (60 miles) along the Kharkhiraa (meaning 'sound of water') and Yamaatiin ('goat') rivers. This route first follows the fast-flowing Kharkhiraa to its upper reaches, taking approximately three days. Glaciers flowing from the twin peaks feed the river, with the Kharkhiraa pass (2974m; 9758ft) making an ideal base camp from which to explore the glaciated side valleys. Mount Kharkhiraa is an easy day-climb for the experienced climber, on ice or rocky snow. From the pass it is a further three-day walk down the Yamaatiin River to the end of this mountain range. In stark contrast to the more populated Kharkhiraa valley, the Yamaatiin valley offers wilderness with deep grasses and summer wildflowers.

Ulaangom (population 29,600), the capital of Uvs Province, is the launching pad for treks in this region, and is a three-hour flight from Ulaanbaatar. Mongolia's domestic flight network is the lifeline for inhabitants in the country's far west, as the alternative to flying between Ulaangom and Ulaanbaatar is a five-day journey by bus on roads that can best be described as tracks. Ulaangom, meaning 'red sand', is a sleepy, tree-lined town spread out along one main street. Horses tied to shop fronts could make one believe that it was the scene for a Wild West movie!

The local market is an excellent place to pick up food supplies, including vegetables, pasta, rice, bread, chocolate and other basic essentials. If you are embarking on a self-supported trek, more exotic ingredients such as salami, muesli, dried milk, and so on are best purchased in Ulaanbaatar. An essential

OPPOSITE INSET *A family portrait – many of the families that inhabit the Kharkhiraa valley in the summer months are from the Khoton ethnic minority.*
OPPOSITE *The spectacular Uureg Lake at the northern edge of the Turgen Strictly Protected Area is one of few freshwater lakes in the region – and great for recuperation.*

TOP *Camels are the main load-bearing animals of Mongolia; one family can usually move their entire household contents, including the* ger, *on just four camels.*
ABOVE RIGHT *The glaciated summit of Mount Kharkhiraa is a popular goal of mountaineers, requiring a vertical ascent of 1000m (3300ft) from the valley floor.*

stop is the local national park's office for local information and to pay the national park's entrance fee, which is usually a rate per person per day.

The small township of Tarialan Soum, a 30km (20-mile) trip by four-wheel-drive southwest of Ulaangom, marks the starting point for treks in the Kharkhiraa valley, as it sprawls along the riverbank. This township is a homeland for the Khoton people, an ethnic minority famous for their special style of dancing, *biyelgee*. It is said that their children are taught to dance at the early age of two – before they learn to ride horses. Tarialan Soum, constructed as an administrative unit in the former communist regime, is a tidy but neglected remnant of those times, boasting a town hall, community centre and school.

The Kharkhiraa River makes an impressive exit from the mountains through a gorge barely 500m (1600ft) wide, between peaks which rise vertically for a staggering 1500m (4900ft). Here the river meanders from side to side between precipitous scree slopes and is, in fact, one of the most challenging sections of the trek. Fed by glacial melt, the Kharkhiraa is waist-deep and fast-flowing, in these lower reaches measuring just 30m (100ft) in width. The combination of the water's depth and volumetric flow makes it extremely challenging to cross except in winter or drought conditions. Locals travel by horse or camel – or 5-tonne trucks carry loads of people across the gorge every few days – as the river is generally impassable by regular four-wheel-drive.

It is possible to negotiate a goat track on foot along the left-hand (southern) bank of the river. This is the recommended approach if vehicles or local herders are unavailable to offer river transport – the consequences of being swept away while tempting to ford the river on foot would be rather undesirable!

After walking upstream for 10km (6 miles) the valley broadens out to more undulating countryside, the river occupying a smaller area of a broader, rocky riverbed. It is practical to continue a further 5km (3 miles) on the southern bank before considering crossing to the northern bank. Fortunately, in the summertime this region is populated by herders, and the possibility of hitching a ride across the river on horseback is good – and makes for great photographs! At this point the northern bank of the Kharkhiraa River forms a broad elevated plateau, safe from floodwaters and ideal grazing land. It is a popular location for herders during the summer months and their white *gers* can be seen dotted along the river edge.

The confluence with the Turgen River requires a ford, however it is relatively straightforward as this river is significantly smaller. After crossing the Turgen, the Kharkhiraa drops beneath the trail and the trek route follows a long U-shaped valley for 20km (12 miles). During summer, the pasture is lush and green, and dotted with the black-and-white shapes of yaks. The trail has gained elevation steadily since the gorge, and is now almost level with the peaks which once towered above it. Here the valley makes a sharp turn northward to reveal a dramatic view of Mount Kharkhiraa and the Kharkhiraa Pass.

After three days' walking, grassy meadows beneath the Kharkhiraa Pass make an ideal campsite and rest point for day-trips in the region. Mount Kharkhiraa is a simple day-climb which, depending on conditions, may or may not require

RIGHT *Mount Kharkhiraa makes an impressive sight as the path of the river swings northwards and its banks broaden out into a distinctly U-shaped valley.*

an ice axe and crampons. The spectacular views from the top sweep across a mini ice plateau which is a tumble of snowfields, glaciers and icefalls – seen from the safety of a grassy campsite. Mount Turgen presents a greater challenge as it is set deep at the end of a tributary glacier of the Kharkhiraa River. There are many smaller peaks, hillocks and valleys to explore.

At this point, trekkers either continue to the Yamaatiin valley or return to Tarialan Soum via the Kharkhiraa River (two days, downhill). The through-trek is a great objective, but logistically it requires arranging a four-wheel-drive pick-up at the trek finish – a very long walk otherwise!

The Kharkhiraa Pass, formed by the glacial moraines of the twin peaks, is broad and flat. Continuing westwards, the trek route crosses an elevated marshy plateau with views across to the Mongol Altai range, some 200km (125 miles) further west. After 20km (12 miles), the route swings northward and rises vertically by 600m (1970ft) to the Yamaatiin Pass, then drops to the Yamaatiin River, which is the direct result of snowmelt off the icecap of Mount Turgen. Its valley makes a great contrast to that of the Kharkhiraa: deep

grasses replace green pastures, and the absence of local herders is evident. This is true wilderness. The valley is the location for active snow leopard research, although it is unlikely that visitors will see this ghostly cat. However, the prospect of ibex and argali big-horned sheep being preyed on is a reality.

The route down the Yamaatiin valley is relatively straightforward; it follows the river's northern bank and crosses many small tributary streams. After a trek of 25km (15 miles), the Yamaatiin River broadens out with shallower sloping banks. This marks the end of the trek – a distance of over 100km (60 miles) has been traversed from end to end.

A final word: due to the remote nature of trekking in this region, it is important that participants are experienced in all facets of wilderness camping, navigation and survival. In alpine environments, snow is possible at any time of year and this should be factored into equipment selection and logistical arrangements. The hospitality of local herders comes as a result of cultural exchange – it can be life-saving at times but should never be relied on, as this ultimately leads to the abuse of local tradition.

ABOVE *The elusive snow leopard has a distinctively short muzzle and high forehead; its tawny coat, with black rosettes, offers effective camouflage in its habitat.*

OPPOSITE *The Mount Turgen icecap in the distance, snowmelt turns the Kharkhiraa River into a raging torrent during the summer months.*

LOCATION Turgen Strictly Protected Area, Uvs province, northwest Mongolia.

WHEN TO GO Summer (June through August). Afternoon rainstorms frequent in summer.

START Tarialan Soum, near Ulaangom, provincial capital of Uvs.

FINISH Lower reaches of Yamaatiin River for through-trekkers, or return to Tarialan Soum.

DURATION 7 walking days (100km; 60 miles).

MAX. ALTITUDE Yamaatiin Pass (3174m; 10,414ft).

ACCESS Domestic flights from Ulaanbaatar to Ulaangom operate three times per week. A vehicle can readily be hired in Ulaangom for the 40km (25 miles) journey to Tarialan Soum. A pick-up at the trek finish should be arranged in advance (although there are no dwellings in this vicinity and trekkers need to be aware of the consequences of a missed pick-up).

TECHNICAL CONSIDERATIONS Of moderate to challenging grade, suitable for experienced walkers of good fitness. Numerous crossings of the fast-flowing Kharkhiraa River required, sometimes needing horse assistance depending on water levels.

EQUIPMENT Sturdy full-leather boots, walking pole(s), Goretex (or equivalent) wet-weather gear (jacket and pants), vest and leggings, four-season tent, four-season sleeping bag, camping stove and cooking utensils. Ice axe and crampons recommended for those interested in climbing trekking peaks along the route.

TREKKING STYLE Wilderness hiking – walking is along well-defined bridle trails mostly in river valleys. These wilderness areas are inhabited briefly by local herders in summer; there is no fixed infrastructure along routes. Trekkers need to be fully self-sufficient. Supported treks are offered by local trekking agencies, and are a recommended alternative to self-supported expeditions due to the remoteness of this region.

PERMITS/RESTRICTIONS A national parks permit is required by all visitors, obtained on arrival in Ulaangom from the local national parks office.

MAPS 1:500,000 (sheet M-46-B) topographic maps are available in Ulaanbaatar.

INFORMATION

Uvs Province Strictly Protected Area Administration, Government Building, Ulaangom, Mongolia; tel: +976-01-45223607.

Karakorum Expeditions Mongolia, Jiguur Grand Hotel, Transport St., Ulaanbaatar; PO Box 542, Ulaanbaatar-46, Mongolia.

website: www.gomongolia.com

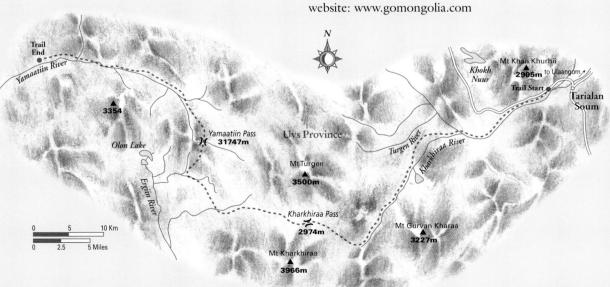

WAY OF ST JAMES

Pilgrimage in the name of a saint

Foot of the Pyrenees, northern Spain
PADDY DILLON

The Way of St James – or Camino (literally, the 'way') – designated the 'First European Cultural Itinerary', is essentially a pilgrim trail. Links from all over Europe lead the faithful onto a final long trek through northern Spain, thus the whole ideal of European unity was forged along its length. It has been walked for a thousand years and has recently seen a revival; those interested in history, art and architecture find it an immensely satisfying route. Although most walkers are Spanish, up to a dozen nationalities can be encountered along the way. It is very well marked, very busy in summer, and a cultural and historical extravaganza from start to finish. Most people walk the route – they are known as *peregrinos* – but many cycle and a few ride on horseback. All are heading for Santiago de Compostela, where St James the Apostle lies buried.

The Way of St James isn't a difficult stretch, but it is long, and very hot and crowded in summer. Spring or autumn are quieter seasons, while winter travel is awkward as many facilities are closed and the higher parts are snowbound. Much of the way leads along clear tracks and paths, with some parts along roads. Hard surfaces mean you should give some thought to footwear – blistered feet are common. Think light and comfortable, and adopt the same for your backpack. Route markings are clear, employing a scallop-shell icon (the symbol of St James) or flashes of yellow paint. A detailed route description is unnecessary, but commentary about features of interest and facilities along the way is useful. While a knowledge of Spanish is an advantage, it is not essential. The local people know why you are here, where you are going, what you need. They have successfully dealt with travellers for a thousand years!

OPPOSITE INSET *The village of O Cebreiro sits on a mountain gap at 1300m (4265ft) in the misty region of Galicia. Don Elias Sampedro ministered here and in recent years worked hard to revive the Way of St James.*
OPPOSITE *Cyclists descend the 'Mulekiller' hill on one of the hottest and driest parts of the Camino, as they head for refreshments in the village of Hornillos.*
TOP *A stone frieze, representing 'Hell', from the Church of Las Animas in the Spanish pilgrim town of Santiago, which is named after Saint James.*
ABOVE RIGHT *Runners, followed closely by two bulls, enter the bullring during the fourth 'running of the bulls' at the annual festival in Pamplona, in 2002.*
PREVIOUS PAGES *Phoenix Bay, looking back towards Loutro, on the Lefká Óri coast.*

PROVINCE OF NAVARRA
Though some walkers cross the Pyrenees from St Jean Pied-de-Port in France, the Way of St James is usually started in Roncesvalles, at the foot of the Spanish Pyrenees. In Navarra – Basque country – the route runs from village to village, among forested hills, then follows the Río Arga. Pamplona, famous for the running of the bulls through its streets in summer, is the first city. There's a gentle climb over the Sierra del Perdon, then tracks lead to Puente la Reina (*puente* is a 'bridge').

Once this fine bridge is crossed, the route heads for the striking hilltop village of Cirauqui. From here, an old Roman road is followed, linking with other tracks to reach Estella. At Irache, thirsty pilgrims can indulge themselves at a public wine fountain.

A long, dry track leads from Villamayor to Los Arcos from where tracks run through fields, vineyards and olive groves, passing the hilltop village of Torres del Río on the way to ancient Viana. Arid country is crossed on the way to the city of Logroño.

PROVINCE OF LA RIOJA

Although the old centre of Logroño is charming and full of character, the sprawling suburbs take time to clear. The Camino passes a nature reserve, where an artificial lake called Pantano de La Grajera attracts waterfowl, on the way to the hillside town of Navarette. Vineyards abound here; La Rioja is where the best wines in Spain are produced. An unpleasant stretch along a road is followed by scenic tracks in rolling hill country on the way to the town of Nájera, which nestles at the base of a red sandstone cliff. The trail crosses through a breach in the rock face and easy tracks lead across cultivated countryside to Santo

Domingo del la Calzada, named after Santo Domingo who is remembered for assisting pilgrims by building a causeway and bridges. The cathedral in this town is a treasure house, full of carved stone and woodwork, richly ornamented, coloured and gilded. There are two awkward stretches of road between Santo Domingo and Belorado.

PROVINCE OF BURGOS

Good paths and tracks beyond Belorado pass many charming villages. Leaving Villafranca, the route crosses the Montes de Oca, passing through oak woods and pine forest before dropping to San Juan de Ortega. A follower of Santo

Domingo, San Juan also built bridges, roads and hospitals for pilgrims. The route wends past picturesque villages surrounded by wheatfields, before reaching a rugged limestone upland that offers lovely views of the city of Burgos. It takes a while to navigate through the sprawling suburbs of Burgos, but the old centre boasts a splendid cathedral.

Rising beyond Burgos is a *meseta* – a high, dry plateau where wheatfields are traversed via long tracks and shade from the blazing sun is limited. Carry plenty of water and check the availability of more ahead, as it takes hours to get from village to village. Hornillos and Hontanas offer shade and refreshments. Castrojeriz, crowned by a ruined medieval castle, is the only large town. Another high *meseta* is crossed before a fine old bridge spans the Río Pisuerga.

PROVINCE OF PALENCIA

The green countryside on the banks of the Río Pisuerga gives way to another dry and barren *meseta* before the Camino reaches Frómista. Here, the church of San Martín is a Romanesque gem. A good path runs alongside a road through the region called Los Campos, and fine villages are passed on the way to Carrión de los Condes, where several historic buildings may be visited. Then a lengthy track crosses open country between Carrión and Calzadilla de

TOP *A statue of a pilgrim in Castilla-y-Leon, in the province of Burgos.*
ABOVE *Walkers cross stubbly wheatfields on the 'meseta' in the blazing sun.*

OPPOSITE *The Camino leaves Cirauqui, perched on a hilltop to keep the surrounding land free for cultivation, via a well-preserved stretch of ancient Roman road.*

LOCATION Along the foot of the Pyrenees, Navarra to A Coruña, northern Spain.

WHEN TO GO Summer (July to August) is very crowded. The route is feasible from March to October, but higher parts may be covered in snow in winter and accommodation becomes scarce.

START Roncesvalles, Spanish Pyrenees.

FINISH Cathedral in Santiago, capital of Galicia (autonomous region of northwest Spain).

DURATION A month on foot or horseback; two weeks by bicycle (800km; 500 miles).

MAX. ALTITUDE Cruz de Hierro, Galicia (1504m; 4934ft).

TECHNICAL CONSIDERATIONS Despite its length, the route is generally easy, provided sensible distances are covered each day. The area is hot and dry in high summer so carry plenty of water and try to find shade to rest in. Set out early to reach the day's destination before it gets too hot. After a *siesta*, enjoy a bit of culture and a meal before nightfall.

EQUIPMENT Walking shoes, trainers or sandals are better than heavy boots (for blisters). Lightweight sleeping bag and mat, lightweight wet-weather gear. In summer, wear cool, light-coloured clothing, a hat and sunscreen and carry a 2-litre (3.5pt) water bottle.

TREKKING STYLE Backpacking, but with ready access to pilgrim refuges and other accommodation. Camping is possible. Most pilgrims walk, but a large number cycle and a few ride on horseback.

PERMIT/RESTRICTIONS No permit is required, but walkers wishing to use the pilgrim refuges should obtain a *credencial* at Roncesvalles and ensure it is stamped daily to prove you are genuinely covering the distance. A fully stamped *credencial* is needed at Santiago to claim the *compostela*.

INFORMATION
Websites: www.csj.org.uk (Confraternity of St James) www.xacobeo.es (official Camino website)
A Short Guide for Pilgrims to Santiago: www.helsinki.fi/~alahelma/santiago.html
Foot by foot to Santiago de Compostela (Judy Foot): foot@naform.freeserve.com

country to Molinaseca, followed by the grim industrial Ponferrada. Several farming villages are passed on the way to Villafranca del Bierzo, where there is a choice of mountain routes: a winding road or a simple track. They join again at Trabadelo from where it is a climb to the village of O Cebreiro (1300m; 4270ft) in the mountains of the Galicia region.

PROVINCE OF LUGO

Don Elias Sampedro, the person responsible for reviving interest in the Way of St James, ministered at O Cebreiro in the mid-20th century. The route uses tracks and paths to descend to Triacastela, with Monte Caldeiron dominating the scene. A choice of routes, left via Samos or right via San Xil, blends into one again in the hilltop town of Sarria, beyond which lie several small villages. Here confusion reigns as names on signposts, maps and guidebooks disagree.

Wonderful winding *corredoiras* (cart tracks) weave between stone-walled fields and a bridge crosses a reservoir to reach Portomarín. The route leaves again by quiet roads over the rugged Sierra Ligonde to Palas de Rei.

PROVINCE OF A CORUÑA

The green countryside between Palas de Rei and Melide is dotted with several little villages. In this area, the Camino frequently crosses a main road that runs from Melide to Santiago; nonetheless, there are quiet stretches along tracks and paths running through eucalyptus forest. Villages are small and simple. Then the trail circles around the airport at Lavacolla to a pilgrim monument on Monte del Gozo.

The final stage is through the suburbs of Santiago, into the ancient city centre and to the imposing cathedral. Enter it via the Portico del Gloria, walk up to a statue of St James and give it a hug, as millions of pilgrims before have done, then descend to the crypt to view the silver casket which holds the bones of the saint. Be sure to visit the dean's house to obtain your *compostela*, a certificate granted to successful pilgrims since the 14th century.

la Cueza. There are several villages, but not all offer food, drink or lodgings, so it is useful to know what's available in advance. Sahagún is the next larger town that offers a full range of facilities.

PROVINCE OF LEÓN

Three churches in Sahagún are classed as national monuments and the town merits exploration. The route continues as a pilgrim path which leads through the countryside beyond. A long line of plane trees stretches into the distance, providing shade in this arid region of rolling wheatfields.

The villages of Bercianos, El Burgo Ranero and Reliegos are oases, offering refreshment and shade. After the town of Mansilla de las Mulas, the landscape becomes more varied as the Camino continues to the city of León. Here, be sure to admire the extravagant stained-glass windows of the cathedral.

As the trail leaves the city it follows quiet tracks across a bleak *paramo* – an arid, scrubby plain where panoramic views can be enjoyed. The *paramo* gives way to cultivated countryside when the Camino crosses a long pilgrim bridge – the Paso Honroso – to Hospital de Órbigo. Small villages are passed on the way to Astorga. Here, there's a fine cathedral and an interesting Museum of the Ways that details the history of the Camino.

A few villages are passed on the wild, scrubby Maragatería. Mountains rise ahead and the climb leads through Rabanal, where the English Hostel is one of the best pilgrim refuges.

After the ruined village of Foncebadón comes Cruz de Hierro, at around 1500m (4920ft) the highest point on the Way of St James, and the route then crosses a ridge to descend via the village of El Acebo, then through mountain

ABOVE *A Galician grain store (known locally as a* horreo*) stands beside a stone house in the Viveiro area of Spain.*

RIGHT *A walker descends from the highest part of the Camino, the Cruz de Hierro, at a height of 1504m (4935ft), towards the little village of El Acebo.*

OPPOSITE *The cathedral in Santiago de Compostela ('field of the stars', or burial place) is journey's end for weary pilgrims – it is the final resting place of St James.*

PICOS DE EUROPA

Pinnacles and limestone boulderfield

Cantabrian mountains, northern Spain
RONALD TURNBULL

The Picos de Europa mountain range, lying in the middle of the Cordillera Cantabrica on the northern Atlantic coast of Spain, is small in map terms. As the lammergeier flies, it measures only 30km (20 miles); it may therefore seem surprising that it has been awarded national park status. This area of limestone towers and rockfields is also sliced by gorges – the Duje River valley and the Cares gorge – which split the range into three massifs: East, Central and West. Very long, steep gullies descend from the heights to river level: the local term used for these is *canal*. The Cares, crossed after the fifth day of the trek featured here, is a kilometre (half a mile) deep. Out of these gorges rise limestone towers and pinnacles, the most famous of which, El Naranjo de Bulnes, is a naked blade of rock some 500m (1600ft) high.

The steep gullies mean you do need to be fit, keep the weight of your packs to a minimum, and make use of the huts and villages rather than rely on self-sufficiency. Even the waymarked hut-to-hut pathways in the Picos are likely to have you clinging to a rock face or crossing a wilderness of holes and boulders while in pursuit of the tiny cairns. Paths confidently lead out to conquer little ledges, swiftly dwindle to a short length marked by fixed cable, then deposit you on a field of forget-me-nots in the middle of a crag.

Between the rock faces and peaks – high above the gorges – the terrain is particularly interesting. Because of its porous nature, limestone doesn't hold water. As a result, the hollows in these hills don't form lakes; instead there is an accumulation of limestone, and the gritty residues of old snow. The rock underfoot is twisted and crumpled, with lots of loose boulders and holes disappearing to who knows where – and yellow paint spots waymarking the trail. The landscape is a mineral kingdom, mainly, but an occasional mimosa or gentian sprouts from a crack, a mountain *rebeco* (the Spanish chamois species) hops across a distant skyline, or a lammergeier wheels, patiently waiting for its prey. In misty weather the Picos are uniquely challenging – the path is no longer visible, when reading the map's contour lines it is impossible to

distinguish between knolls and hollows, and what appears to be level ground turns out to be a maze of little crags. In clear weather, the limestone simply slashes your boots, wears away your fingertips and renders your legs very, very tired.

Trekkers choose the Picos because they haven't been developed and groomed for tourism. So be prepared for the closing of shops during *siesta* which lasts the entire afternoon. Food is basic – bread and cheese – and the local *cabrales*, or goat's cheese, is as challenging as the limestone pinnacles above the towns! Further, be forewarned that English is not spoken. And waymarks have weathered to faded yellow paint at unreliable intervals, while 'fixed' cables are not necessarily all that firmly fixed. As adventure treks go, the Picos de Europa is not among the tame ones!

To start the trek, Arenas de Cabrales is easy to reach by bus from the coast road through the ferry port of Santander. It has *pensiones* and a camping ground, and useful shops – your last chance to stock up on gas cylinders for the camp stove. The first day over the Sierra de Portudera to the village of Sotres is technically straightforward but still demanding. Start early to escape the heat. A cobbled path, reputedly Roman, rises for 1000m (3300ft) through sweet chestnuts to a bleak area of rock and pasture. Waymarks are sparse, but incorrect routes are recognized by their thorn-scrub and scree. At the Collado Posadoiro Pass, the jagged skyline of the Picos appears with heart-stopping suddenness across the deep green hollow of the Duje River – or Río Duje.

The little village of Tielve has dirt streets and ancient tiled houses. A road leads up the valley towards Sotres; an old mule-path above the village on the left offers a more interesting way up. This preliminary day can be cut out by taking a bus or local taxi.

OPPOSITE INSET *Mountain huts in the Picos are inexpensive, basic and friendly. This one is at Collado Pandebano, on the way up to Urriellu.*
OPPOSITE *Such remote, rugged terrain makes it quite evident why Bulnes is one of the last villages in Europe to remain inaccessible by road.*

TOP *Simple, rustic dwellings such as these in Tielve, passed on the first day of the trek, typify the village character of the Picos.*
ABOVE RIGHT *The strange-looking Veronica hut. The Torre de los Horcados Rojos, above, is very much easier to ascend than is apparent from this viewpoint.*

The second day is a circular tour of the Eastern Massif, so the heavy back-packs can stay at Sotres. After a walk up through old lead mines to Collado Valdominguero, you embark on a superb rocky ridge walk and scramble, with serious drops alongside, but there is no real difficulty. Robin Walker's guide-book indicates a rock-climbing descent into the col before Pico del Jierru, but there is an easier way slightly left of the crest. The circuit continues over bare rock slabs that are warm or even hot under the hand, and along a sharp rock-ridge. On the right is a drop of 1800m (6000ft) into the blue haze that fills the Valdebano. Final summit is the Pico del Sagrado Corazon ('the peak of the sacred heart'). In keeping with the peak's name, the summit cairn holds a statue of Jesus inside.

The third day is technically the most demanding. It follows the Río Duje past Vegas de Sotres to ascend the Canal del Vidrio. This gully harbours a rock slab that's gently angled and easy, but rather exposed, with loose scree. This unpleasantness is worth it, as the ground rises in chunks and ripples of twisted limestone to eventually reach a 10m-wide (33ft) pass between two rock needles – Collada Bonita, whose entirely apt translation is 'lovely little pass' You then drop into a gully of scree and boulders, and work around the base of the spectacular Naranjo de Bulnes, for an inexpensive supper of soup and sausage at the Urriellu hut.

Behind the hut is a peak, which despite its 500m-high (1640ft) tombstone appearance is a straightforward scramble along a ridge of sun-warmed rock with an eagle floating by and a heat-hazed valley an awful long way below your right-hand boot.

An alternative route for the day (from Sotres to Urriellu) is an undemand-ing one on tracks and paths by way of the Collado Pandebano.

On day four, the route continues southwards through two distinctive lime-stone hollows, the Jou Sin Tierre and Jou de los Boches. A section of easy scrambling, assisted by a fixed cable, leads to the Horcados Rojos Pass. Leave backpacks here for a straightforward but 'airy' ascent of 2506m (8220ft) Torre de los Horcados Rojos.

The distinctive Veronica hut is the turret from a World War II aircraft car-rier, brought in by helicopter. It serves refreshments and sleeps three. But an even finer nightspot is ahead. First comes a stony mule track where the worst obstacle is a cow-pat - or you may have to stand aside to make way for the cows themselves. A short side-trip leads to Pico de la Padiorna – a straightforward summit, apart from the obligatory 300m (1000ft) drop on the other side. The main path continues across a stony plateau, but then suddenly descends over the edge, to where an astonishing ledge path runs horizontally halfway up a precipice. And at its end is the hut at Collado Jermoso, perched on a scrap of meadow high above the Cares gorge.

On the following day, the 1200m (3940ft) descent to Cordinanes takes much longer than you expect. Even so, you should reach Cain early enough for a side trip down the Cares gorge. This is the one part of the trip that could be called a stroll, on a wide path through tunnels carved out of the rock wall

LEFT *The carved-out path above Cares gorge is spectacular, but wide and smooth; in this trek of the Picos it is viewed as an 'easy' stretch.*

RIGHT *Jermoso hut on its tiny meadow high above Cares gorge; to the left is the Torre del Friero.*

LOCATION Parque Nacional Picos de Europa, in the Cordillera Cantabrica of northern Spain.

WHEN TO GO Best time is June and September. July and August are hotter, more crowded, and afternoon thunderstorms are more frequent. Snow from October to May (can persist into June).

START Arenas de Cabrales; has a bus link to Llanes for trains and long-distance coaches to/from Santander, Bilbao.

FINISH Covadonga; has bus links to Arriondas for coach and train.

DURATION 7 days (105km; 65 miles).

MAX. ALTITUDE Horcados Rojos Pass (2344m; 7690ft); Torre de Horcados Rojos (2506m; 8220ft).

TECHNICAL CONSIDERATIONS A tough trek involving some scrambling, difficult route-finding and ascents/descents of 1200m (4000ft).

EQUIPMENT Lightweight leather boots (limestone destroys fabric ones); warm clothing items and lightweight wet-weather gear; tent or shelter, sleeping bag and mat (unless pre-booking huts); 2-litre (3½pt) water bottle and daytime meals (huts serve basic evening meals and breakfast); Spanish phrase book.

TREKKING STYLE Hut-to-hut walking. Urriellu hut is busy and Jermoso is small. Huts can be prebooked (via Tourist Info at Potes); alternatively carry lightweight sleeping gear (bivvy bag) in the hope that if the weather turns foul, there will be room in the hut.

MAPS 1:25,000 by Adrados Ediciones.

PERMITS/RESTRICTIONS No permit is required. Lightweight camping/bivvying is accepted around huts and above 1600m (5250ft); there are campsites at Cain and Lagos de Enol. Otherwise no camping permitted within the national park.

INFORMATION

Websites: www.tourspain.es; www.picoseuropa.net
www.liebanaypicosdeeuropa.com/in
www.alsa.es (coastal coaches)
Tourist Information Potes,
fax: +34-942-730787.
National Park Info Centre,
tel: +34-985-849154.
Tourist offices Arenas/Cangas,
tel: +34-985-846484 or 848005.

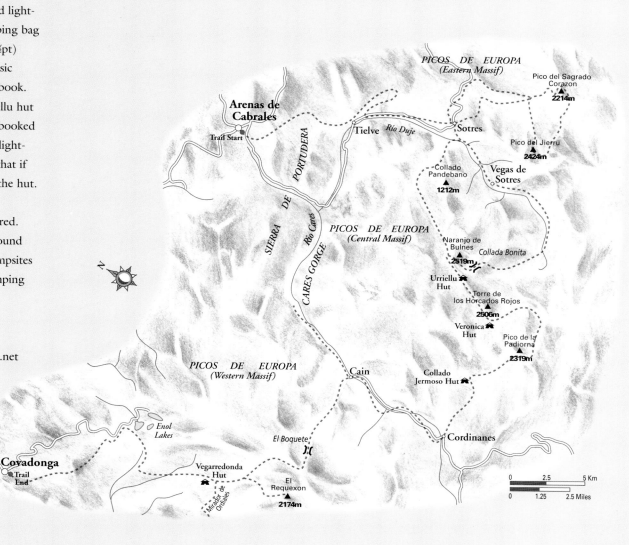

(the gorge splits the Picos range from north to south). However, it has 100m (330ft) drops, no handrails, and bridges that even the Spanish admit are a bit dubious. You won't have time to follow this spectacular gorge all the way – it eventually emerges on the southern side of the range. Return to Cain for its *pensiones*, camping field and useful shop.

By day six you should be fit enough to face the 1500m (4920ft) climb into the Western Massif. A zigzag path takes you up steep meadows and between crags to the narrow entrance called El Boquete. Once through this 'little mouth' you're swallowed up by the hugest of the limestone hollows, the Jou Santu. It leads through the Picos range's high peaks to the Vegarredonda Hut.

How you spend your final morning will depend on your energy. Two hours away there's El Requexon, which offers a short but exposed rock scramble. Once up its rough, sunny limestone you linger above tremendous empty spaces. In one direction, the jagged silhouette of the mountains resembles the cardiogram of an agitated heart; in the other, grey rock foreground fades into blue, then green, reaching halfway to Santiago.

Alternatively you can visit Mirador ('viewpoint') de Ordiales, which has a vista that's half as spectacular – the sheer drop is on one side rather than both – but involves no rock scrambling. Or you could simply lie around in meadows of Christmas roses, occasionally buying another beer from the hut…

The journey ends with a wander down to the Enol lakes (Lagos de Enol), then across the cow meadows of Vega las Traviesas and down through woodland to Covadonga. This is the sacred capital of Spain: it has a cathedral, a cave waterfall, and a chapel tucked under an overhang like a swallow's nest. It's a place as surprising, and inspiring, as the Picos themselves.

LEFT *Water of any sort is scarce in limestone country, so coming across Lago de Ercino on the final day strikes trekkers with some surprise.*
ABOVE *The trek ends at Covadonga, whose chapel nestled into the cliffs marks the site of a local girl's vision of the Virgin Mary.*

111

NORTH PINDOS MOUNTAINS

Travelling the ancient mule paths

Northern Mainland Greece

JUDY ARMSTRONG

Forming the central spine of mainland Greece, the Pindos mountains stretch southward from Mount Grammos on the northwest border with Albania to the Gulf of Corinth. From above, this highland range resembles an extravagantly wrinkled tablecloth dotted with stone villages, wooded forest, limestone towers, deep gorges, and some of Greece's highest mountains. In the days before roads were built, the mountains were so remote that even the Ottoman tax collectors avoided the region!

Within the vast tracts of the Pindos, the best known area for trekking is in the north, in the district of Zagoria, where trails, including several international long-distance paths, have been waymarked. Zagoria, which directly translates as 'the place behind the mountains', has been inhabited since the ninth century BC. Because of its early isolation, it became wealthy and autonomous, a situation that prevailed until the 20th century, when wars and economic migration caused the decline of many villages.

Today, a sensitive approach to ecotourism is helping revive many villages, yet the area remains remote and untouched. In 1990 the Vikos-Aóos National Park was created within the Pindos range. It is home to European bear, wild boar, lynx and wolves but these animals are elusive and rarely seen.

A six-day trek takes in the best parts of the North Pindos, including a breathtaking walk down the world's deepest gorge and exploring an alpine plateau – which can provide more excitement than you bargained for! Two ethnic groups, the Vlachs and the Sarakatsani, traditionally graze their sheep on the high mountain meadows; their dogs are large and loud – and trained to protect their flocks at all costs.

The trek can be reduced to four days if ascents of the Gamila and Astraka peaks are excluded, plus the walk to the historical village of Vradheto.

Distances each day are short so that time can be spent absorbing the views and dozing in the shade. This leaves plenty of scope for side excursions, and for sampling the menus of the village tavernas. Each village has one or two

guesthouses which offer, besides their excellent food, friendly hospitality (a Greek-English phrasebook will be a valued addition to your luggage).

The best starting point for this trek is the timeless village of Vitsa or its neighbour, Monodendri. Like most Zagorian villages, they are built almost entirely from local stone: the softer white rock comes from quarries, the harder black stone from rivers.

Monodendri, on the lip of the Vikos gorge, is home to the uninhabited monastery of Ayias Paraskevis and secret caves where hermits and persecuted Christians laid low in centuries past. Today, the monastery offers both serenity and wide-angle views into the gorge.

The descent into Vikos gorge passes a Guinness Book of Records sign informing trekkers of the measurements for this 'deepest gorge in the world' – but the figures are given the wrong way around! It is the depth that is 1650m (5410ft) and the width, 980m (3215ft). The track down to and along the gorge was greatly improved in 1998 and it is now virtually impossible to get lost. Walking it is delightful, through maple and walnut woodland, along tracks fringed with wild thyme, and over gigantic boulders on dry sections of the Voidhomatis riverbed. Wildflowers bloom, cicadas rasp and tortoises amble slowly across the track. As the gorge sweeps around bends, views change constantly, surrounded by skyward-soaring cliffs.

The climb to Vikos village (called Vitsiko on some maps) follows the switchbacks of an ancient *kalderimi*, or cobbled mule track, up the gorge side. Once the sole domain of mules and their drivers, the maintenance of these amazing tracks now benefits from European Union grants.

The village of Vikos is perched on a breeze-cooled saddle, with sweeping panoramas on all sides. Watching the sun set outside the Pension Vikos guest-

OPPOSITE INSET *Dramatic dry-stone bridges spanning rivers and canyons in the limestone district of Zagoria date back to the 18th and 19th centuries.*
OPPOSITE *Looking north along the Vikos gorge, from the Beloi viewpoint near Vradheto. Cut by the Voidhomatis River, it is claimed to be the world's deepest.*

TOP *Despite the dry summers, river water is abundant in the Pindos mountains; natural swimming pools are fed by springs gushing from canyons.*
ABOVE RIGHT *A hiker trekking through the Vikos gorge; a waymarked path – No. 03 – follows the canyon floor, offering easy walking in breathtaking scenery.*

house, eating baked feta cheese and rich meatballs washed down with local Mythos beer is paradise indeed.

The next day's route follows the hairpin bends of the *kalderimi* on its way to the village of Mikro Papingo and twists back to the river. It passes a white chapel before reaching the Voidhomatis spring. Here, ice-cold water takes a week to drain 1300m (4250ft) through the cliffs.

Once over the river, the climb up to Mikro Papingo is steady for about two hours, with far-reaching views and glimpses of caves. Wild strawberries grow on banks and green lizards sunbathe on pebbles. Nearer the village, trekkers' eyes are drawn upward to the Pirgi, or Papingo Towers, which loom like giants over the track. Like most of the Zagorian villages, Mikro ('small') Papingo and its sister Megalo ('big') Papingo, have the status of protected traditional communities, meaning that their architectural integrity should be maintained. This is certainly true in Mikro Papingo, with its narrow cobbled lanes, tightly packed stone houses and stone-flag roofs. Walking from here to Megalo over the old Zagorian arched bridge, an architectural delight in a limestone gorge, includes an opportunity to swim in the deep, natural pools of the river. Back at the Pension Dias, a very comfortable if quirky guesthouse, you

can eat marinated olives and drink local white wine, watching the village goats being herded home for the night along quiet, cobbled streets.

On day three, the morning's climb from Mikro Papingo soon moves above the tree line, with rural Greece spread below. The Astraka cliffs, striped with snow gullies well into June, dominate the view. It's a three- or four-hour hike up to the Astraka Refuge, a white building on a windy pass at 1950m (6397ft). The main hut, owned by the Hellenic Alpine Club, offers basic accommodation but the location is magnificent. From the terrace a path runs down a bouldered bank, skirts a pond and huts used by shepherds in summer, crosses an alpine meadow, then climbs to Dhrakolimni – 'dragon lake'. Legend relates of its bottomless depths, in which its guardian dragon lives. Vivid blue gentian flowers grow on the lakeshore, and the surrounding cliffs are reflected in the cold, deep water.

Next day it's time for some real height gain, up Gamila I (2497m; 8192ft) and Astraka Peak (2436m; 7992ft). Of the several approaches to Gamila, the shortest follows a thin trail across a limestone plateau at the foot of the Astraka cliffs. The mountains visible on the left are Ploskos (2377m; 7799ft),

TOP *A wild iris, photographed at the head of Megas Lakkos gorge. Home to eagles as well as wildflowers, this gorge intersects the southern end of the mighty Vikos.*

ABOVE *Lakes named after dragons always have legends attached, and the unfathomable abyss of Drakholimni is no exception.*

Gamila I and Gamila II. A lone tree is the signal to turn left into a shallow valley which leads up to Gamila I. A steady hike up its broad flank leads to the flat, rocky summit with views across the Aóos River valley to Mount Smolikas (2637m; 8651ft), the second highest mountain in Greece.

Climbing Astraka involves backtracking from the huts toward Papingo, then weaving left around the cliff edges while following cairns to the summit. The wilderness appears enormous – this is a remote, timeless place – and reinforces the extent of Greece's montane and uninhabitable land.

Setting out on the fifth day from the Astraka Refuge, the trail passes Gamila, skirts little lakes, crosses alpine meadows and files down bands of limestone rock. Now the upper reaches of the Megas Lakkos gorge are visible and the path drops into the gorge, then climbs up the left bank, under steep cliffs and past banks of wild iris. It looks as though eagles should live here, and apparently they do. Well waymarked, the path climbs out of the gorge when the walls narrow in anticipation of its meeting the Vikos gorge, then crosses grassy hilltops and streambeds before descending a meadow to the village of Tsepelovo. This is a stone enclave on the edge of the mountains, snowbound in winter and a cool haven in summer. Men gather in the main square to play backgammon while the women stay indoors. Pension Alexis Gouris is a hub for visitors to Tspelevo, with its balconies, courtyard and friendly welcome. From here begins the final day's walk to the village of Vradheto and back.

Starting on a poorly maintained *kalderimi* leading up the right side of a deep ravine, it is the old route to the village which until recently was only accessible by foot. The climb is steep, through limestone bands and across grassy bowls. It arrives, suddenly, on a shiny new road – the ancient track has been sealed for the final 4km (2½ miles) to Vradheto. Luckily a track leaves this road, heading for the Beloi viewpoint over the pancake rock stacks of the Vikos gorge. With Monodendri behind your left shoulder, you can look along the length of the gorge, Vikos village faintly represented as a clutch of grey buildings. The scale is terrific and it's a treat to see the entire route in context.

Vradheto itself, just half an hour away, is a very small village with an active taverna. Its claim to fame is a *kalderimi* called the Vradheto Steps. This plunges through a rock palisade in a complicated series of twists and turns to a Zagorian bridge – and the modern road back to Tsepelovo.

ABOVE *The massive limestone buttresses of the Papingo Towers, also called Pirgi of Astraka, create a formidable backdrop to the village of Mikro Papingo.*

ABOVE *The Vradheto Steps, an old* kalderimi, *until recently the only access to the village of Vradheto.*

OPPOSITE *The icy water of this Voidhomatis spring pool takes a week to seep through the 1300m-high (4250ft) cliffs.*

LOCATION The northwest corner of mainland Greece, near the border with Albania.

ACCESS International flights to Preveza airport (approx. 2.5 hours' drive from Vitsa village); or fly to Corfu and transfer to Igoumenitsa by ferry. Buses connect Preveza and Igoumenitsa with Ioannina, the area capital, which also has a local airport. There are regular bus services from here to Zagoria villages.

WHEN TO GO May and June (best for wildflowers), September and October. The alpine areas are snow-bound in winter.

START Vitsa or Monodendri (adjacent villages), North Pindos mountains.

FINISH Tsepelovo, North Pindos.

DURATION 4–6 days (covering 60km; 37 miles).

MAX. ALTITUDE Gamila 1, one of Greece's highest peaks (2497m; 8192ft); or Astraka Col/Refuge (1950m; 6397ft), if the ascent of Gamila is not included in the route.

TECHNICAL CONSIDERATIONS Some difficulties may be encountered on the alpine section, around Gamila, early in the season (May and early June); this would be impassable without skis or snowshoes in winter. Although the Pindos mountains are close to the Albanian border, this does not impact on visitors in any way except that accurate (military) maps are not available.

EQUIPMENT Walking boots, backpack, layered cloth-ing to cope with temperature extremes (it can be scorching hot in the gorge and snowing near Astraka). Walking poles are useful for steep descents. Wilderness camping is illegal – and guesthouses offer a Greek slice of life that should not be missed.

TREKKING STYLE Backpacking on a well-marked trail, with the option of ascending two peaks. Paths are marked with red paint on rocks and trees indicating the 03 national trail for most of the route, with blue and yellow markings in the final stages. You need to be fairly fit, and enjoy walking in wild surroundings. Route finding is usually straightforward. There are plenty of climbs and descents, but paths follow the most sensible lines so even gaining height is fun. Guesthouses in isolated villages and the mountain hut on Astraka Col provide comfortable accom-modation and excellent food. Guided and self-guided walks with luggage transfer also available.

MAPS Maps from the Hellenic Alpine Club (from *Korfes* mountaineering journal), with contour intervals at 200m (655ft), have been adapted from the 1:50,000 military series, sheets 55–60.

PERMITS/RESTRICTIONS None.

INFORMATION

Ioannina EOT (tourist office), Napoleonda Zerva 2, Ioannina.

National Tourist Office of Greece, 4 Conduit St., London W1R ODJ.

Adventure Center, 1311 63rd St, Suite 200, Emeryville, CA 94608; tel: +1-510-6541879; fax: 6544200.

Websites:

www.sherpa-walking-holidays.co.uk
(Sherpa Expeditions; provide all transfers).

www.adventure-center.com/Explore

ACROSS THE SPINE OF CRETE
A path less travelled

Eastern Mediterranean, Greek Isles
CHRISTOPHER SOMERVILLE

Looking back, it's hard to say which tormented me more as I stood on the pebbly beach at Káto Zákros at dawn on Easter Monday: the hangover, or the apprehension. The hangover would soon be gone; it had been generated by the Greek Orthodox celebrations of Easter – always at their most ferocious here in Crete – into which I had enthusiastically, if injudiciously, plunged from the moment of my arrival on the island a week before.

The apprehension was of a different order and not so easy to brush aside. I was about to tackle the toughest hurdle of my walking life – to travel the entire length of the Mediterranean's largest and most mountainous island along the European Path E4, which starts in Portugal and crosses various central and eastern European countries (there are 12 long-distance European Paths that form a network covering the whole continent).

The E4 is a seldom-travelled track. From all I could gather, it might not even exist any longer. Those few people back in England who had heard of the E4 had muttered darkly about poor waymarking, bad maps and lengthy 'lost' sections among some of Europe's trickiest mountains and gorges.

I faced other problems, too, that first morning. The supposed route, somewhere between 400 and 480km (250 and 300 miles), led not through Crete's tourist-friendly coasts and beach resorts but across four mighty mountain ranges: Thripti (1476m; 4843ft), Dhikti (2148m; 7048ft), Psiloritis (2456m; 8058ft) and Lefká Óri (2453m; 8048ft), which form the backbone of the dinosaur-shaped island. In this remote high country of dialect-speakers, my lack of all but a few phrases of Greek looked likely to be a formidable handicap.

I had already discovered that guidebooks to E4 did not exist. What skimpy knowledge of the route I possessed had been gleaned from members of the Greek Mountaineering Club in Iráklion – keen mountain-goers, and helpful, but not too reassuring. The only map available, a German 1:100,000 double-sheeter, was too small-scale and vague to give me much in detail or encouragement. What it did show was a scattering of agricultural villages and hamlets

along the E4 route (a thin red line wriggling from one end of Crete to the other), thinning out in the high mountains to large blank areas with only isolated shepherds' huts by way of human habitation. Overnight accommodation was clearly going to be a matter of bed if lucky, sleeping bag if not.

During my first five days of westward walking I covered about 110km (70 miles) and got myself over Thripti, the first and lowest of the four ranges. Overnight stops included one spartan and one superb bed-and-breakfast, a small hotel, a village room where rats danced in the water tank all night, and a turn in my trusty sleeping-bag on the veranda of a friendly taverna owner – a selection that was fairly typical.

In Kritsá, a big mountain village, I holed up with Cretan friends for a few days to nurse 11 spectacular blisters. Crete's rugged mountain paths are unforgiving to the unprepared foot, but this was as bad as it got. Within a couple of weeks the soles of both my feet had grown to resemble cratered yellow rubber, stank like goats, and were impervious to anything short of a sharp nail.

My spoken Greek improved rapidly, through force of circumstance, so that the halting 'Good mornings' and 'Thank yous' of Káto Zákros soon grew into whole sentences. By the time I had crossed the still frost-bitten Lassithi plain in the company of young Cretan mountaineer Pantelis Kampaxis, and had descended from the Dhikti mountains into the rolling olive and grape country behind Iráklio, I could ask for directions and understand the replies – shakily, but serviceably enough. It's wonderful what a fortnight among monoglot locals will do.

By this time, I had stopped fretting about finding direction and overnight accommodation, initially my two biggest worries. The Cretans I met in the mountain villages and among the vineyards and olive groves were endlessly

OPPOSITE, INSET *Donkey rides take visitors up to Psiloritis to see caves that, according to legend, are the birthplace of the Greek god, Zeus, supreme ruler of all gods.*
OPPOSITE *Samariá gorge, 1800m deep (6000ft) and 13km (8 miles) in extent, is just one of a dozen such canyons in the Lefká Óri, or White mountains.*

TOP *On the coast of Sfakia, the white houses of Loutro lie tightly curved around their roadless bay beneath high mountain walls.*
ABOVE RIGHT *The cloth sails of the Lassithi plain's irrigation wind pumps were a classic sight on Crete before electricity and diesel ousted the simplicity of wind power.*

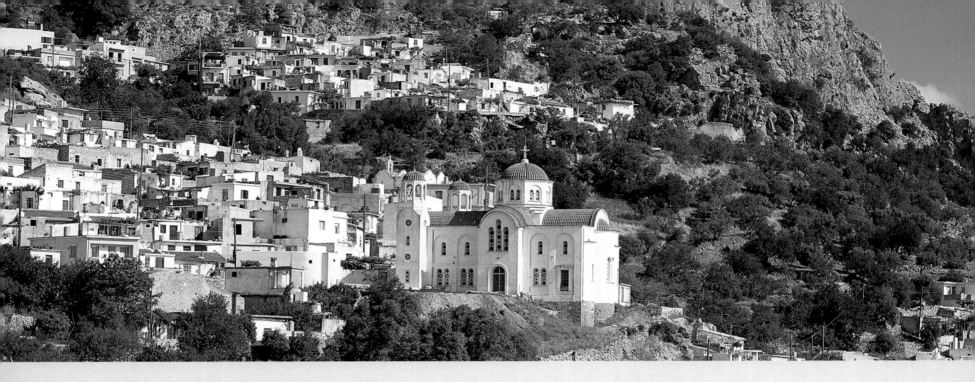

LOCATION Crete, eastern Mediterranean, Greece.

WHEN TO GO April to May are best for flowers, celebrations (Greek Orthodox Easter and First of May) and weather (not too hot) – but the path through the White Mountains (Lefka Ori) may be snowed up until June, necessitating the coastal alternative.

START Káto Zákros (eastern Crete).

FINISH Hrissoskalitissas (western Crete).

DURATION Approximately 1 month (400–480km; 250–300 miles).

MAX. ALTITUDE Psiloritis (2456m; 8058ft).

TECHNICAL CONSIDERATIONS The route is supposed to be marked with yellow and black signs on poles, but many have been removed or shot full of holes; some are misleadingly placed. Binoculars are essential for spotting distant E4 waymarks.

Summers are very hot, so it is essential that you carry sufficient water.

The three trickiest sections, where all lone walkers except very experienced mountaineers may need a companion or guide, are: Katharo plain to Lassithi, and Lassithi to Kastamonitsa; crossing Psiloritis; and crossing the White Mountains.

EQUIPMENT Wear proper hiking boots (the Cretan terrain shreds anything flimsier). A sleeping bag is essential. Other useful items are a Greek phrase book, light binoculars, basin plug (generally lacking in hikers' accommodation!), soap, washing powder and clothes pegs (for all that dirty washing!).

TREKKING STYLE Solitary, unguided backpacking; need to be self-sufficient for those nights between villages where no accommodaton is found. Bigger towns and villages have hotels and rooms for rent. In smaller ones try the taverna or *kafenion* (café) owner, *pápas* (village priest), *tháskalo* (schoolteacher), or mayor

– there's always somewhere to lay out your sleeping bag. The locals are very hospitable, and it is generally possible to find a meal. This is adventure trekking because of a distinct lack of maps and guidebooks.

PERMITS/RESTRICTIONS No permits required.

MAPS These are sketchy. The best available is Harm's Verlag's 1:100,000 2-part map of Crete with the E4 marked in red. Also, the *Crete Trekking and Road Map* in 4 parts by Giorgis Petrakis (available in Crete bookshops, or by mail from Planet International Bookstore, Odos Chandakos, Iráklion.

INFORMATION

The Greek Mountaineering Club (EOS), Odos Dikeosinis 53, Iráklion 71201; tel: 227609 (opening hours 20:30–22:30, Mon–Fri). Will mark your maps, advise you and arrange guides if required. Website: www.explorecrete.com/hiking.html

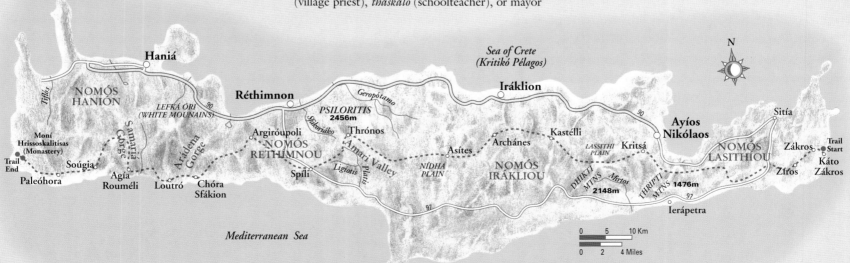

helpful and boundlessly hospitable. Philoxenia, they call it – love of the stranger – and to me it came in the form of a drink of cold well-water, or an orange offered on a hot road, a finger politely pointing out the path, a bowl-ful of snails and steamed herbs, or a bed for the night freely offered with no refusal accepted. When I could not find a room – a rare occurrence – I slept under the stars in the warm, clear, Cretan spring nights.

I had the companionship of Pantelis Kampaxis, too, when I climbed Psiloritis, the highest peak in Crete at over 2450m (8000ft). Viewing the mountain from the Nídha plain the night before the climb, its majestic whale-back gleaming with moonlit snow and whistling with rising winds, my chick-en heart quaked. But Pantelis is the kind of man who will scale such a moun-tain with nonchalance and then go for a 30-mile run to get some exercise ...

By noon the next day I had slogged up through the snowfields after his stringy, lightly built figure and was crouched in the drifts on the summit,

whipped by a freezing gale, with the whole of Crete laid out below like a glorious relief map. The exhilaration was a celestial slap in the face.

I came down from Psiloritis into the Amari valley in need of a little lazy time, which turned into two weeks of idling, so seductive were the drowsy delights of the lush green Amari in spring. Wildflowers carpeted every hillside, bees buzzed in the sage. In every village, tiny Byzantine churches opened their

OPPOSITE *The big mountain village of Kritsá, nestled below the Dhikti mountains, is the home of some of Crete's most hospitable and knowledgeable mountaineers.*
ABOVE LEFT *Trekkers plod down the zigzag* kalderimi, *or cobbled pathway, that plunges dramatically into the Arádena gorge.*
ABOVE *The formidable White mountains, snowcapped even in summer, rise like breaking waves at the back of the Sfakiot village of Anopolis.*

doors to disclose frescoes painted 500–600 years before – masterpieces of religious conviction, humorously and lovingly depicting rural life on the island.

At the Taverna Aravanes in Thrónos, perched high at the top of the valley, I had a breathtaking view of Psiloritis from my balcony and idled the days away chatting, writing poems and learning to play the Cretan *louto* – a big-bellied bouzouki-like instrument.

Every country has its centre of traditional music, and Amari is Crete's. More expressive than the *louto* is the *lyra*, a three-stringed fiddle held across the knee and bowed with such fervour by Kostis, Antonis and the other village musicians that people would come crowding whenever they were moved to play. *Protomayiou*, the first of May, saw the maddest of celebrations, a Dionysian feast of roast lamb and wine under the trees where lyras squeaked, singers roared like lions and pistols cracked skywards.

Feet recovered, strength restored and a desire for the road rekindled, I hoisted my pack at last one morning and turned my back on Amari. It was west again, looking in vain for elusive E4 waymarks on invisible poles, following dirt roads and old cobbled shepherds' tracks when E4 forsook me, and drawing a little closer each day to the ultimate obstacle: Lefká Óri, the White mountains. The climbers of the Greek Mountaineering Club had been dubious about my chances this early in the year. Melting snow was lying in fragile bridges over hidden sinkholes, and most of the E4 signs had been removed by unwelcoming shepherds. It was the sinkholes that finally sank any prospect of a crossing, on the incontrovertible advice of the mountaineers.

The E4 divides at this western end of Crete. The low road, no less spectacular than the high, took me up and down a succession of awe-inspiring gorges in the final weeks of May. Samariá gorge, far-famed for its depth of 1800m (6000ft), had the highest walls and the biggest crowds, but it was the sneaky sidewindings and huge boulder slides of the Arádena gorge that nearly did me in when I all but toppled over a steep rock face after getting lost.

I celebrated my 50th birthday in the quiet coast town of Loutró, reading back through the journal I had kept and only half believing the adventures recorded there. Journey's end came after a few days of slippery but beautiful coastal walking above a turquoise Libyan Sea. On Whit Sunday eve, seven weeks after setting out from Káto Zákros, I limped into Hrissoskalitissas, the Monastery of the Golden Step. Father Nektarios, its wild-haired solitary monk, gave me raki and sweet biscuits as a greeting, and showed me to a cell where I slept round the clock. Next morning he woke me with a vigorous clanging of the monastery bell.

Legend says that one of the steps that ascend the rock of Hrissoskalitissas is made of gold; only the pure in heart can see which one it is. As I climbed up towards the blue-roofed church to give thanks for fears overcome and lessons learned on this most remarkable of walks, I kept a hopeful eye out for it. But all I saw was thick May sunlight, gilding the flight from bottom to top.

OPPOSITE *If followed in the opposite direction to that of this walker, the coastal path leads to Sweetwater, a splendidly isolated beach situated west of Chora Sfakion.*
RIGHT *Hrissoskalitissas, the Monastery of the Golden Step, appears at journey's end like a great white ship riding seas of olive groves.*

THORSBORNE TRAIL

Towering massifs and translucent waters

Hinchinbrook Island, Queensland, Australia
SVEN KLINGE

Australia has hundreds of gorgeous tropical islands – but Hinchinbrook stands out for its sheer scale, isolation and sense of wilderness. It must rank with Lord Howe Island as one of the most beautiful in the Southern Hemisphere. Located off the northeast coast of Queensland, approximately halfway between Townsville and Cairns, and separated from the mainland by the narrow Hinchinbrook Channel, it offers idyllic beaches, sheltered coves, fresh-water pools and mountains that tower over the island. From lofty vantage points along the east coast, walkers are rewarded with vistas of sweeping bays interspersed with rugged headlands.

Declared a national park in 1932, Hinchinbrook (39,000ha; 98,600 acres) is the largest island-national park on Earth. It is also a protected natural site as it lies within the Great Barrier Reef World Heritage Area.

The Thorsborne Trail, which traverses the island's east coast, is named after the late Arthur Thorsborne who, together with his wife Margaret, had a life-long interest in nature conservation, which included the monitoring of Torresian imperial pigeons.

At least four days are required to walk the minimum of 32km (20 miles) between Ramsay Bay in the north and George Point in the south. It is recommended that hikers spend a longer period than this on the island, with a rest day at the mid-point of the trek, either at Little Ramsay Bay or Zoe Bay. An extra day or two will also be needed to complete a spectacular side trip to Mount Bowen. While the Thorsborne Trail can also be walked north from George Point, it is commonly walked the other way around, and prior arrange-

OPPOSITE INSET *Hikers relish easy open walking on the beach at the southern end (the finish) of the Thorsborne track on Hinchinbrook Island.*

OPPOSITE *The Mount Bowen massif, a sharply delineated ridge of dramatic spires and formations, captures the dawn light over the Warrawilla lagoon.*

TOP *The moist, wet conditions in the swamps of the Zoe Bay catchment area are an ideal habitat for the tall palm-dominated rainforest.*

ABOVE RIGHT *Hikers gain access to the northern end of Hinchinbrook Island by boat, to start walking the world-famous Thorsborne Trail.*

PREVIOUS PAGES *Hikers on the Liebig range, which separates the Murchison and the Cass valleys. To the right is Aoraki/Mount Cook, to the left Mount Sefton.*

ment with a boat operator is necessary for the journey to Lucinda. Here, a shuttle bus can be taken back to Port Hinchinbrook. Navigation along the trail is easy, as there are orange-coloured triangular markers every few hundred metres. The side trip up the summit of Mount Bowen is quite difficult, however, as the route is not indicated by any trail or markers, therefore experience is necessary. If you do decide to include this, walk from Ramsay Bay to Little Ramsay on the first day, from here to Mount Bowen (return) on the second, to Zoe Bay on the third, then from here to Mulligan Falls the following day, and to George Point on the fifth and final day.

The walk starts in an inspiring way with a ferry trip across Hinchinbrook Channel, then through a labyrinth of mangrove-lined estuaries to arrive at the Ramsay Beach. For most visitors, it is quite an unusual experience to arrive by boat *behind* a beach. Even as you are coasting through the dense mangroves, there are impressive views to the Mount Bowen massif, with Nina Peak dominating the foreground.

Head right (south) to the end of the beach where the trail is cut through open eucalypt forest, over a ridge to Black Sand Beach. It is here, with the jetty out of sight, that you get your first sense of isolation. The vast Pacific Ocean fills your vision to the east and looming over you to the west is the spine of the

Mount Bowen upland. From Black Sand Beach, head immediately inland and steeply up towards Nina Peak (312m; 1024ft). At the ridge crest, drop your packs for a steep ascent up a signposted trail to the summit, about 1km (½ mile) return. The views on the approach are outstanding, especially at the topmost point looking towards the north over Ramsay Bay and east towards Mount Bowen. It is best to climb early in the day so that you avoid the haze from sugar-cane burning.

The trail then descends to Nina Bay. Seasonal water is generally available behind the small lagoon between January and August. A creek at the southern end of the beach also provides a source of fresh water. There are campsites and a pit toilet here, one of the few attempts at infrastructure on the island.

The next camping area is at Little Ramsay Bay where fresh water may be collected at a creek a few hundred metres up from the Warrawilla lagoon.

On day two, it is from here that the most popular route up to Mount Bowen (1121m; 3678ft) commences. It is a difficult return walk to the summit, so allocate a full day. You might also want to rest the next day to recover. With no track and over a kilometre of height to be gained, most walkers find it lengthy and exhausting.

You should leave very early (at first light) and follow the creek upstream. This primarily involves boulder-hopping, which makes progress painstakingly slow. Be careful on the boulders as many are loose – even the very large ones – and severe accidents have occurred. It is important to judge carefully which fork to take when the trail branches; forks are marked by rock cairns and they are generally to the right. Along the way, there are some wonderful pools to tempt walkers into a rewarding and refreshing dip. After about three or four hours along the trail, the flowing water dries up as the creekbed climbs steeply upwards. Make sure you keep on the creekbed until you reach the saddle. If you have taken a wrong turn, then return to the camp at midday otherwise you will run out of daylight hours.

From the narrow spine, head left up onto the rocky ridge-crest where a pronounced track heads over several false bluffs to the summit, marked by a cairn. There are great 360-degree views of the island's dramatic mountain landscapes, including the sheer bluff of The Thumb. Islands dot the coast to the north and south, while to the west the Great Dividing range looms over the rainforest and sugar-cane fields of the mainland. Return via the same route. Campsites on the massif are limited, and not ideal, so try to avoid carrying an overnight pack, which limits progress.

From Little Ramsay Bay on day three, continue south past more white sandy beaches, then inland through open forest, cool dark rainforest and mangroves to North Zoe Creek. While the warning signs at the creek crossing warn that estuarine crocodiles may inhabit the area, they fail to give advice as to how to react when you do disturb one ... there is actually little one can do except run! In reality, attacks are rare, but it is best not to linger in the area.

LEFT *South Zoe Creek forms a series of cascades down the rocky slopes of Mount Diamantina, creating a series of freshwater pools to cool hot hikers.*
ABOVE RIGHT *Taking in the view west from Nina Peak to the rocky ramparts of Mount Bowen's east face, the highest peak on Hinchinbrook Island.*

LOCATION Hinchinbrook Island, off the coast of north Queensland, Australia.

WHEN TO GO The tropical climate makes it imperative to visit in the dry season (winter), between April and September.

START Ramsay Bay, northeast Hinchinbrook.

FINISH George Point, southeast Hinchinbrook.

DURATION 5 days (49km; 30 miles), which includes side trails. Actual trail is 32km (20 miles).

MAX. ALTITUDE Mount Bowen (1121m; 3678ft).

TECHNICAL CONSIDERATIONS Some navigational difficulties ascending Mount Bowen (optional) – there are no signs or a track.

EQUIPMENT Walking boots; sandals for sand-walking and creek-crossing. Sleeping bag, mat and tent. Fuel cooking stoves (gas or liquid); no campfires permitted. Food must be stored in ratproof containers. Sunblock and insect repellent are essential. Water bottles, as there are sometimes many hours between freshwater sources. A GPS receiver for the Mount Bowen ascent is useful.

TREKKING STYLE Comfortable coastal and sand walking on a well-marked and signposted track. Walkers must be self-sufficient and carry their own tents; camping is in designated areas only.

MAPS Highly recommended are the AUSLIG Cardwell 1:100,000 and SUNMAP Hillock Point 1:50,000 topographical maps.

PERMITS/RESTRICTIONS A permit is needed for the Thorsborne Trail; only 40–45 hikers are permitted on the island at any one time (the largest group size is six members). Stricter guidelines apply for the Mount Bowen ascent; permits may be difficult to obtain as only two parties per month are permitted to summit. All arrangements need to be booked beforehand, including the ferry from Port Hinchinbrook and to Lucinda.

DANGERS Saltwater (estuarine) crocodiles have been known to inhabit the North Zoe Creek area, so be alert. Box jellyfish are highly poisonous and appear between May and October; don't swim in the sea if they are present. Be aware of dehydration and heat exhaustion in the tropical heat; drink plenty of water. Carry tide tables for Lucinda to enable safe crossings of estuaries.

INFORMATION

Rainforest & Reef Centre, 142 Victoria St., Cardwell, Queensland; PO Box 74, Cardwell QLD 4849.
Booking permits: tel: +61-7-40668601.
Port Hinchinbrook ferry: tel: +61-7-40668270.
Lucinda ferry: tel: +61-7-47778307.
Websites: For Queensland parks, www.env.qld.gov.au/environment/park
For ferry times and bookings, www.hinchinbrookferries.com.au

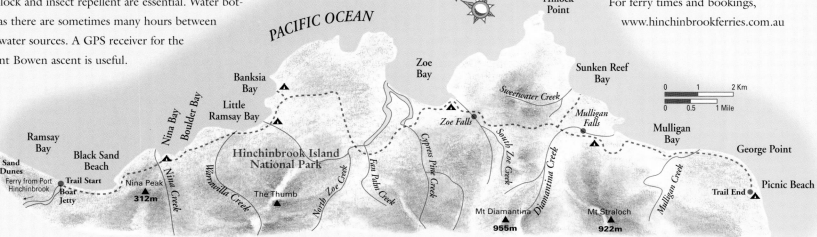

This inland section of the Thorsborne Trail is relatively flat and progress is rapid. From North Zoe Creek, the trail crosses several smaller creeks, making it necessary for walkers to remove their boots as the water can be deep and fast-flowing, making rock-hopping impossible. Drinking water can be found at Fan Palm Creek.

Once at the delightful Zoe Bay, the campsites are located at the southern end of the beach, hidden in the forest. There are several marked areas together with a pit toilet. Native rats can be a hazard here – take care that they don't damage backpacks and tents in their attempt to get at food. A metal box is provided here for protection. Evidence of the rats can be seen on fallen coconuts that have holes gnawed through them!

On leaving Zoe Bay on the fourth day, the trail initially runs parallel to South Zoe Creek before fording it approximately 100m (330ft) downstream from Zoe Falls. This waterfall and its turquoise pool are worth seeing; they are

assuredly one of the most picturesque sights on the island. An interesting pastime is to feed the eager fish after swatting the abundant flies! The seclusion, clarity of the water and surrounding tropical landscape make this the most perfect of oases. Camping is not permitted here.

The trail files to the left of the pool up a steep slope onto granite slabs above the falls. Some ropes/chains have been installed here to ease the climbing. Another pretty pool is located at the top, where walkers usually jump in for another cooling swim. After following South Zoe Creek, the trail climbs a distinct spur to a granite rock pavement marking a saddle. This spot 263m (863ft) above sea level is the highest point of the Thorsborne Trail, not including any side trips. From here on, it is fairly heavy going as it descends into several steep gullies that drop perpendicular to the track. This can be very tiring and progress is slow as you constantly have to descend, then ascend again. The trail leads down into the Diamantina Creek catchment, passing on the way a signposted side track to Sunken Reef Bay – which is good for a swim. The detour takes about 30 minutes each way and there is an informal camping area at the beach. Water may be available up a small creek at the northern end, but should not be relied on.

ABOVE *From this position, gazing across one of many swimmable freshwater rock-holes above Zoe Falls, the views out to Zoe Bay and the Coral Sea are glorious.*

Continuing on the Thorsborne Trail, follow the markers diagonally across Diamantina Creek. The track runs up a short slope before descending a steep hillside to reach the base of Mulligan Falls – another picture-postcard natural pool lined with boulders and rock ledges. Note that the rock pavements above the falls are extremely slippery and dangerous; signs warn walkers not to venture there.

The camping area is located about 100m (330ft) from Mulligan Falls and is popular because of its proximity to George Point. Tent sites are formally segregated. Once again take precautions against native rats eating into packs and tents. It is advisable to suspend food from a wire tied between two trees. Having plastic bottles rotating on their longitudinal axis at each end of the wire prevents the bushrats from walking along the wire, as they fall off when they try to cross the turning bottles.

On your fifth and final day, fresh water should be collected before leaving Mulligan Falls as it's about 7.5km (4½ miles) to George Point. The trail continues a further 2.5km (1½ miles) through picturesque open rainforest and

crosses five creeks. The last, Moth Creek, provides fresh water seasonally but should not be relied on. The trail comes out of the vegetation at the northern end of Mulligan Bay Beach, which is exposed to prevailing winds from the south. A park sign denotes the track entrance about 300m (1000ft) south of Diamantina Creek inlet.

George Point, the southern end of the trail, is a further 5km-walk (3 miles) south along the beach and progress can be tiring across the soft sand and into the strong headwind. Note that there are no signposts along this section. Two-thirds of the way along, Mulligan Creek flows into the bay. It is advisable to cross this creek at low- to mid-tide otherwise the currents could prove dangerous. There are some excellent views of the two peaks, Mount Diamantina and Mount Straloch. The latter features the wreckage of an American B24 Liberator bomber which crashed here in 1942.

With the final leg of your trek now behind you, while waiting for the ferry you can hone your outdoor skills by attempting to extract the coconut milk out of a freshly fallen husk.

TOP *To cope with Queensland's intense tropical heat, estuarine crocodiles adjust their body temperature by means of this fierce-looking, open-jawed grimace.*

ABOVE *Having crossed a broad creek mouth at Mulligan Bay, a hiker rearranges his backpack before setting off for George Point and the trail end, an hour away.*

Central Southern Alps, New Zealand

SHAUN BARNETT

A 600km (370-mile) spine of glaciated mountains divides New Zealand's South Island down its entire length. Although not high by world standards, the peaks of the Southern Alps (Ka Tiritiri o te Moana is the range's Maori name) are nonetheless dramatic as they rise so close to the ocean – at Āoraki/Mount Cook to almost 3800m (12,500ft) only 30km (18 miles) from the coastline. Glaciers, including the Franz Josef and Fox (both of which almost reach the sea), cover much of this region. To the west of the Alps lie deeply gorged valleys and dense rainforests; to the east are dry windswept grasslands and broad braided rivers.

Two national parks form the boundaries of the central Southern Alps: in the south is the Āoraki/Mount Cook National Park and in the north, Arthur's Pass National Park. While both are very popular and accessible locations for climbers and hikers, it is the remote and little-visited stretch of countryside in between that offers the ultimate scope for adventure on long-distance transalpine hikes. Depending on the route taken and the weather encountered, trekkers will face a number of challenges and need to be prepared for glacier travel, river crossings and, in places, bush navigation.

On the western side of the Alps travel is undoubtedly slower, wetter and more difficult, but here lie some of the more spectacular landscapes, including the Bracken Snowfield, and the Garden of Eden and Allah ice plateaus. Hiking in the east is generally faster, but moraine and riverbed travel here can be tiresome, and several of the major rivers, the Rangitata and Godley in particular, may be difficult to cross. A fast party will need a minimum of 10 days to complete the eastern route, but two to three weeks is more likely, and if you intend spending time on the western side of the Alps, allow up to four weeks.

Climbers have been tackling long traverses in the central Southern Alps from as early as the 1930s. In December 1934, GCT Burns and Max Townsend were two of the first to complete a trip, when they crossed eight passes with ascents covering more than 7800m (25,590ft) between Arthur's Pass and Āoraki/Mount Cook in just 13 days. More recently, in 1989, Michael Abbot

completed an astonishingly bold solo traverse not just of the Southern Alps, but 1600km (990 miles) along the entire South Island in 130 days.

These days there are usually only one to two attempts per year. Most parties begin in the north at Arthur's Pass where travel is easier and there are few glaciers. However, late in the season snowmelt makes rivers very difficult to cross, and opening crevasses can make glaciers impassable, so it may make more sense to tackle the bigger, more glaciated country of the south first (the route described is in this south-north direction, and covers a mixture of travel in both the west and east). This traverse begins in Mount Cook village. Towering above the village is the immense pyramid of Mount Cook, or Āoraki – 'the sky piercer' – the highest of New Zealand's mountains (3754m; 12,317ft). From this village, hikers face two options, both involving travel up glaciers. Most choose the Tasman glacier, at 29km (18 miles) New Zealand's

OPPOSITE INSET *Approaching Barker Hut in a blizzard, Arthur's Pass National Park.*
OPPOSITE *Āoraki/Mount Cook, the pinnacle of the Southern Alps, towers over the Tasman glacier – New Zealand's longest.*

TOP *Frozen blocks of snow caused by the glacier breaking apart as it travels.*
ABOVE RIGHT *A hiker receiving unwanted attention from several kea – the world's only alpine parrot, and an endemic species of the South Island.*

longest, while some opt for the Murchison glacier, the second longest. While the Tasman offers more travel on white ice and less on gritty moraine, trekkers will eventually have to cross into the head of the Murchison regardless. Both routes begin with the milky-white Tasman glacier terminal lake, discoloured from glacier-ground mica. Both valleys are surrounded by some of the country's highest mountains, and make an impressive – if daunting – introduction to the trip. At this angle, Āoraki/Mount Cook appears as a giant parallelogram with two massive glaciated faces dominant, while the ice peak of Mount Tasman has two prominent shoulders that at times look like a white bird with wings poised, ready for flight. From the head of the Murchison glacier (two to three days' trekking) several routes into the Godley valley exist, but the most used are the Classen and the Armadillo Saddle. Both will require good climbing and navigation skills, and in the wrong conditions may prove impassable. In the Godley valley, lying in the north of Āoraki/Mount Cook National Park, the silvery ribbons of the Godley River merge and divide to form striking patterns on the broad valley floor. From here, there is really only one option: a crossing of Terra Nova Pass at the valley head. Getting there, however, may well be the hardest part of the trip. Rain or snowmelt can easily make the Godley uncrossable, and there are no bridges. However, good huts provide basic accommodation to wait out bad weather.

Many glacier meltwater lakes in the Southern Alps are increasingly challenging to get around; most have grown considerably with recent glacial recession. By far the best option for traversing the Godley glacier terminal lake is to sidle around the true right (to the left-hand side, facing upstream), but this requires fording the Godley River once again. Sidling around the true left avoids crossing the river, but rockfall and steep bluffs make this very dangerous. A high route over nearby highground is possible, but will require dextrous navigation and good weather. Terra Nova Pass leads from the head of the Godley glacier, under the imposing helmet of Mount D'Archiac, eventually into the Havelock branch of the Rangitata River, which is liberally laced with small but welcome huts (about a week's trekking will have elapsed). St Winifred's Hut is a good spot for your first 'food dump' – due to the trek length, you will need to organize a helicopter operator to fly in food supplies on two or three occasions.

The Havelock and especially its neighbour the Clyde are very large rivers and can only be crossed during periods of low to medium flow. Hikers should be well versed in river-current crossing techniques, and never attempt fording alone or when the water level is high. During the early days of high country farming, drowning in such rivers was so common that for a while it was known as 'the New Zealand death'.

Loose rock is another danger. By now hikers will be familiar with the easily shattered greywacke and schist rock that makes up so much of the Southern Alps. The grinding of the Pacific and Indo-Australian continental plates has uplifted New Zealand's relatively young mountains over the past five million years, raising them a total of 18,000m (59,000ft) – over twice the height of Everest. However, the sedimentary layers of these mountains are eroded at

RIGHT *A lone trekker negotiating the moraine wall between the Murchison and Tasman valleys, in the Āoraki/Mount Cook National Park.*

much greater rates than the rock of the Himalaya, hence their more modest stature. From the headwaters of the Clyde, it is possible to traverse the Gardens of Eden and Allah, immense ice plateaus straddling the western side of the Alps. They offer transalpine hiking par excellence, and are likely to be the highlight of your trip. From Perth Col at the head of the Frances valley, access onto the plateau is reasonably straightforward so you can strike out across the glistening plateau roped-up for glacier travel. All is ice and snow, and the silence profound. There are stupendous views back to Āoraki/Mount Cook and north to the lesser known but equally inspiring peaks of Whitcombe and Evans.

However, difficulties multiply when getting off the plateau into the Wanganui valley. The Adams River is very tough bush-crashing along a very sparsely marked route, while the adjacent Lambert glacier and gorge are impassable. Routes do exist allowing trekkers to sidle around treacherous loose-rock and tussock slopes onto Lambert Spur between the two valleys. Once down in the Wanganui valley, steep banks are clothed in dense forest and the turquoise-coloured river rushes through gigantic schist boulders. Another week will have passed. A marked route of sorts exists upriver, but this is tough going, and parties choosing this route will be thankful to reach Smyth Hut (and its natural hot pools!) near the valley head after one to two days.

The Rakaia valley (where parties can rejoin the eastern route) is reached from the Wanganui after crossing the Bracken Snowfield, a striking area of flat, crevassed glacier beneath the precipitous 'cloud-gatherer', Mount Evans, followed by a descent down onto Whitcombe Pass. Like other passes in the Southern Alps, the Whitcombe Pass was once a route for Maori travellers crossing the divide in search of *pounamu*, or greenstone – a treasured type of jade used for weapons and ornaments. Nowadays, the tracks and huts of the Whitcombe valley provide a useful way to make progress directly northward. These huts, many of them built in the 1950s and 1960s, provide shelter from the often unpredictable and stormy New Zealand weather. Rainfall on the West Coast is amongst the highest in the world – one year, a tributary of the Whitcombe recorded a staggering annual rainfall of 16.6m (54ft).

From Whitcombe Pass it takes two to three days to travel to Frew Hut; Arthur's Pass is just a week away. Valley-hopping from Frew Hut over Frew Saddle leads to the Hokitika River; from here Mathias Pass is crossed to the Mathias River. Crossing the Rolleston range to the Wilberforce River, the not-so-distant mountains of Arthur's Pass draw perceptively closer. The upper reaches of the Wilberforce River offer several choices for reaching the boundary of Arthur's Pass National Park, among them Whitehorn Pass or White Col. Both lead into tributaries of the Waimakariri River, one of the major valleys of Arthur's Pass. It is also here that the trip concludes, at Klondyke Corner. Your legs will be weary, but you'll have walked some 250km (160 miles), and crossed in excess of 10 passes, through truly demanding terrain.

OPPOSITE *Two hikers climb out of the Havelock valley; rising prominently on the horizon is Mount D'Archiac.*
ABOVE RIGHT *With Mount Kensington rising dramatically behind them, trekkers make their way across Mount Tyndall via the Garden of Allah ice plateau.*

LOCATION Central Southern Alps, New Zealand.

START Āoraki/Mount Cook Village.

FINISH Klondyke Corner (Arthur's Pass).

BEST TIME TO GO The summer months (December to January) are probably best, although in winter (July to September) ski-touring trips are possible.

TREKKING STYLE Full self-reliance is required; there are some tracks, and huts in most of the major valleys, but these are not often present on the high ground. Huts are basic – bunks, mattresses, and wood stove. A modest charge is payable to the Dept. of Conservation.

TECHNICAL CONSIDERATIONS Expect to encounter flooded rivers, glaciers, high alpine passes and lots of moraine; only people with considerable transalpine hiking experience should attempt this. You'll need a helicopter fly-in to 'dump' at least one food supply – probably two or three.

EQUIPMENT Tough transalpine boots, crampons, ice axe, rope and glacier travel equipment;

alpine tent and sleeping bag; thermal clothing and storm gear; gas stove, cooking utensils and food. It is also advisable to hire a mountain radio for regular weather forecasts and for emergency purposes.

TWO SUGGESTED ROUTES

West and east mixed route (allow 3–4 weeks)
Āoraki/Mount Cook village, Murchison glacier, Classen Saddle, Godley valley, Terra Nova Pass, Havelock River, Clyde River, Frances valley, Perth Col, Garden of Eden, Garden of Allah, Lambert Spur, Wanganui River, Bracken Snowfield, Whitcombe Pass, Whitcombe River, Frew Saddle, Mathias Pass, Rolleston range, Wilberforce River, White Col, Waimakariri River, Klondyke Corner (Arthur's Pass).

Eastern route (allow 2–3 weeks)
Āoraki/Mount Cook village, Murchison glacier, Classen Saddle, Godley valley, Terra Nova Pass, Havelock River, Clyde River, McCoy stream, McCoy Col, Rakaia River,

Ragged range, Mathias River, Rolleston Range, Wilberforce River, White Col, Waimakariri River, Klondyke Corner (Arthur's Pass).

MAPS A series of 1:50,000 detailed topographical maps by Terralink NZ are ideal for the entire trip.

DANGERS Rockfall, flooded rivers, avalanches, and crevasses all present dangers. The weather is notoriously unpredictable, and fast-approaching storms with rapidly falling temperatures and winds gusting up to 150kph (90mph) are not uncommon.

INFORMATION

Alpine Guides (Mount Cook) Ltd, Ring Road, Mount Cook Alpine village, tel: +64-3-4351834; fax: 4351898; e-mail: mtcook@alpineguides.co.nz website: www.alpineguides.co.nz

Mount Cook National Park, Visitor Centre, PO Box 5, Mount Cook, tel: +64-3-4351819.

Adventure Consultants/Guy Cotter, e-mail: info@adventure.co.nz; website: www.adventure.co.nz

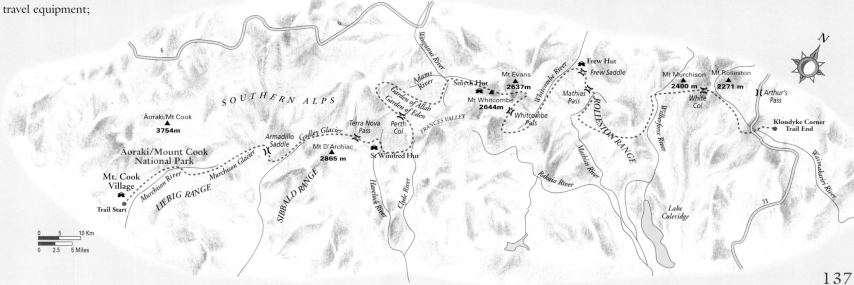

AFRICA

NORTHERN DRAKENSBERG
Crossing the barrier of spears

KwaZulu-Natal, South Africa
TOM HUTTON

The Drakensberg, literally translated from the Afrikaans language as 'dragon mountains', form the very spine of South Africa. Running north to south for over 200km (125 miles), they create a natural border between the province of KwaZulu-Natal and the tiny mountain kingdom of Lesotho, and offer endless opportunities for adventurous trekking.

The route discussed here, which will take a fit walker five days to complete, winds its way along the escarpment edge at the northern end of the range. Starting at the mighty Sentinel, in the Royal Natal National Park, it passes some of the 'Berg's (as it is known to those who've climbed it) most famous landmarks: the Devil's Tooth, the Amphitheatre, Icidi Buttress, the Fangs, the Saddle, the Bell, and of course, the magnificent Cathedral Peak. Along the way it traverses rugged, often trackless, terrain; slips back and forth across the Lesotho border; crosses the sources of some of the country's mightiest rivers; and then ends each day in the shelter of a hidden cave.

The scenery throughout is awesome. Away from the escarpment edge, the landscape is barren and austere with only the occasional rocky peak or tumbling mountain stream to mark the way. But, after frequent forays across this impressive plateau, the trail repeatedly returns to the real spectacle – huge and broken basalt cliffs, adorned with needle-sharp pinnacles and knife-edge arêtes, that thrust up from the fertile hills of the Lowberg, lying at times over 1000m (3300ft) below.

The trek starts from the Sentinel Office of the national park, where permits can be obtained. A good track heads from here up towards the escarpment

edge before tailing out into a narrow path that zigzags beneath the mighty Sentinel rock-tower. The views improve with every step and the climbing is made a lot easier by the distraction of the scenery to the north, towards the formidable walls of the Amphitheatre and the instantly recognizable spire of the Devil's Tooth.

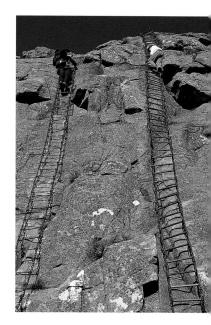

The track then traverses the flanks of the Sentinel before terminating in a dark and narrow cleft in the hillside. Here you take the much written-of, intimidating-looking chain ladders, up two levels, onto the plateau beneath Mont-aux-Sources. The path, slightly fainter at this stage, then heads southeast to the infant Tugela River. Follow its course gently down to the escarpment edge and stop to take in the full grandeur of the Amphitheatre from the top of one of South Africa's most impressive waterfalls (it tumbles for 948m; 3110ft).

From this point onwards, the trek takes on a much wilder flavour as you leave the good paths behind and make your way across significantly more rugged terrain. Head south, to pick up a tributary of the Kubedu River, and follow this downstream to a major confluence. Where the waters meet, you turn left and follow the second tributary uphill, pretty much due east, back onto the escarpment near the Ifidi Pass. Continue above the pass, where you'll see the dramatic Ifidi pinnacles, and then head due south to cross over the back of the Ifidi Buttress. This time you'll rejoin the escarpment close to the Icidi Pass where you'll spend the night. The cave is little more than a shallow overhang on the northern side of the pass.

From Icidi, the route continues south, behind the Icidi Buttress, before dropping to cross another of Kubedu's tributaries. Continue in the same direction; pass around the right of a small hill and then drop to another river. The best route heads east from here, back onto the ridge line, for a great view over the rock needles of Madonna and her worshippers. Stay on the escarpment edge now, cross the top of Fangs Pass and then veer southeast to pick up yet another river. Head upstream, still southeast and then, as the river meanders

OPPOSITE INSET *A hiker stands atop an outcrop in the Mnweni Pass. In places, the escarpment drops over 1000m (3300ft) to the fertile lands of the Lowberg below.*
OPPOSITE *The narrow plume of the Tugela falls, viewed from the top of the Amphitheatre in the Royal Natal National Park.*
TOP *The rock overhangs that form the Mnweni Cave, one of the finest overnight stops in the Northern Drakensberg.*
ABOVE RIGHT *These daunting-looking chain ladders lead, in two stages, up onto the plateau near the Mont-aux-Sources Amphitheatre.*
PREVIOUS PAGES *A bitter, icy wind blows unhindered at the summit of Kilimanjaro – as myriad ice-crystal formations inside Kibo Crater testify.*

south, bear off to the left to locate the Rwanqa Pass. Day two's not quite over yet; drop down the pass for approximately 300m (1000ft) and then scramble up to the cave in the cliffs on the right. The cave, considerably more comfortable than Icidi, is often frequented by baboons that, unlike their tamer cousins which frequent popular tourist spots, will make a hasty exit upon catching your scent. Other wildlife frequently seen along this section of the 'Berg includes rock hyraxes, or dassies, as they're more commonly known, and buck such as the largest of the antelopes – the eland – and also the smaller grey rhebuck.

The third day starts with a short climb back up the pass where a track leads west, down to the river again. Follow this southward and then, to avoid losing too much height, head southeast, back onto the clifftops near Pins Pass. The escarpment swings around to the east here and the views across the next section, above the Mnweni Cutback, are among the best of the whole trek. The Zulu people named the Drakensberg *Quathlamba*, meaning, literally, 'barrier of upright spears', and as you gaze along the escarpment from the top of Pins Pass, it's easy to see how formidable this barrier must have appeared.

Continue south, following the line of the Lesotho border, over a rounded but distinct ridge and then contour around – first to the east and then to the northeast, to regain the clifftops near the wonderfully named pinnacles of Eeny, Meeny, Miny and Mo. The best line now heads due east into the Senqu

ABOVE *Hikers above a chasm in the Amphitheatre wall; from this elevation, the Tugela falls drop 614m (2000ft).*

ABOVE *Frequently seen gliding along the escarpment edge, the beautiful bearded vulture, or lammergeier, has a wing span of over 2m (6½ft).*

valley, where you'll cross the source of the Orange River before climbing back up above the Mponjwane Tower (also known as the Rockeries). This is the domain of Cape vultures. Much maligned, these beautiful birds colonize the rocky towers along the escarpment and use the considerable updrafts created by the cliffs to glide effortlessly over the plateau edge searching for food. From close quarters it's possible to hear the wind in their wings and their calls echo eerily back from the surrounding rocks. They share the Drakensberg skies with black eagles, more solitary birds with deep and heavy wings, and with the much rarer lammergeier, or bearded vulture, a stunning mountain dweller easily recognized by its diamond-shaped tail. Head south from the tower and track back onto the plateau slightly to round some rocky outcrops. Here, you'll locate a trail of cairns that will take you back onto the escarpment and down to the Mponjwane Cave, which, perched on a broad ledge, is probably

the most spectacularly situated shelter of the whole tour. Sunrise from the cave is something that shouldn't be missed, but day four is a long one so break camp and head off as early as you can.

A faint path heads south from the cave to the Rockeries Pass. The views across the jumble of rocky promontories and pinnacles are breathtaking and you should be able to make out the distinctive profile of the Bell, close to your finishing point yet still some way off in the distance. From the Rockeries, head southwest, away from the edge, where you'll pick up the Orange River once again. Follow this down to its confluence with the Koakoatsi and then back-

ABOVE *Looking down Rockeries Pass to the valleys of the Lowberg; the seemingly impenetrable escarpment wall is breached by a number of similar weaknesses along its length.*

track to trace the meandering course of this river, almost due east, towards the Nquza Pass. Here, the river is channelled by a distinct valley that runs south to north and a pronounced ridge runs along its western side. Climb this, making your way through the occasional rock band and then descend by contouring around to the west, again avoiding rocky outcrops and small crags. The escarpment is regained above Ntonjelana Pass and from here, the trek follows the edge, as closely as possible, to Cathedral Peak. On the far side of the peak is the Mlambonja Pass, your final descent route. Follow this down into a saddle where you'll see another track leading down to the left. It ends in the relative luxury of Twins Cave, one of the largest and most popular of the 'Berg shelters. The views back along the escarpment to the north are really quite something and it's easy to make out the Devil's Tooth, so close to your starting point, four days earlier.

The final day is spent descending but there's no time to relax just yet. The path is tricky in places and there's an awful lot of altitude to lose before you finally reach civilization. The first task is to take the trail back up to the

Mlambonja Pass. Once reached, this is easily followed as it mimes the course of the river down into a lush green valley where colourful ericas and proteas come in stark contrast to the barren mountain scenery you've grown accustomed to over the last few days. In places, the trail can be confusing but the way is normally marked by a small cairn, perched precariously on a large boulder, somewhere close to hand.

At the 2000m (6560ft) mark, the trail splits. The right-hand option is generally considered the better one. This contours for a while before climbing again and finally zigzagging steeply down to flatter ground. Soon after this, the trail leaves the Mlambonja Wilderness Area behind and picks up a way-marked track that leads down to the Cathedral Peak Hotel.

ABOVE *The source of the Senqu/Orange River, Mnweni.*
OPPOSITE *The Tugela River, iced over, on the plateau above the Amphitheatre. Here, at 3000m (10,000ft), winter can be a harsh time to cross the Drakensberg.*

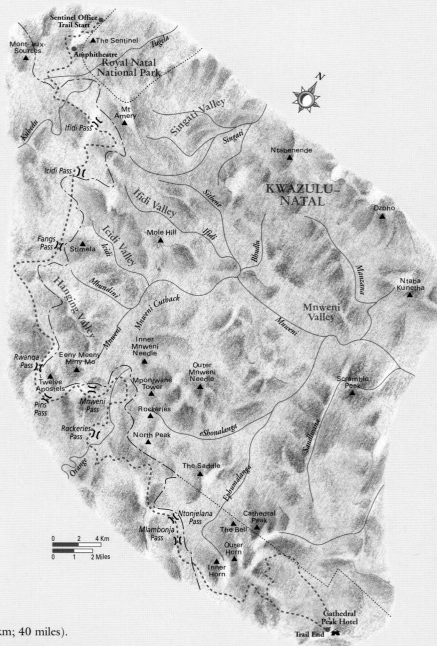

LOCATION Northern Drakensberg mountains, KwaZulu-Natal, South Africa.

START The Sentinel carpark, Royal Natal National Park.

FINISH The Cathedral Peak Hotel.

TREKKING STYLE Backpacking across a mainly untracked crossing of exposed high mountain plateaus following the edge of a rugged and rocky escarpment. Apart from water, which is available from the rivers, all food and supplies must be carried.

WHEN TO GO April and May (autumn/fall), June (winter), September and October (spring) or November (early summer) are generally considered the best months. Winter is drier but any precipitation at that time can fall as snow.

DURATION 5 days (approx. 65km; 40 miles).

MAX. ALTITUDE Escarpment edge (3400m; 11,155ft).

TECHNICAL CONSIDERATIONS No climbing involved but proficiency in navigation and a good understanding of general mountain knowledge are required.

EQUIPMENT Good three-season walking boots, waterproof/breathable jacket and long pants, thermal underwear, summer clothing items such as shorts for the middle of the day which can be hot any time of year. A 3- or 4-season sleeping bag and mat are essential and a bivouac bag is an advantage in the caves.

MAPS 1:50,000 maps available from the KwaZulu-Natal Nature Conservation office.

PERMITS/RESTRICTIONS

A permit can be purchased from the national park office at the start of the trek.

DANGERS Weather is extremely fickle in the Drakensberg: a hot summer's day can produce a midday thunderstorm with lightning, dense fog can roll in, a crisp frosty winter morning can turn into a blinding snowstorm. Come well prepared.

INFORMATION

KwaZulu-Natal Nature Conservation Services, PO Box 13053, Cascades 3202, KwaZulu-Natal, tel: +27-33-8451000/2.

Website: www.southscape.co.za

MOUNT KILIMANJARO

Snowpeak on the equator

Tanzania, East Africa
STEVE RAZZETTI

Kilimanjaro, the highest peak in Africa, lies just south of the equator in north-eastern Tanzania. Its singular snowcapped mass soars majestically above the Maasai steppe, and with grazing giraffe and elephant in the foreground, it presents a spectacle that is quintessentially African.

The ascent of 'Kili', as it is affectionately known, is today one of the most popular mountain excursions in the world, and certainly makes for an unforgettable climax to an East African adventure.

The very notion that there could be snow on the equator was ridiculed by the geographical establishment when missionaries Ludwig Krapf and Johann Rebmann returned from their travels there in 1848. However, it was soon established that Kilimanjaro was close to 6000m (19,700ft) in height, and on 5 October 1889 German geologist Hans Meyer, with alpine specialist Ludwig Purtscheller and local guide Jonas Louwa, succeeded in reaching the summit. With typical colonial arrogance he named the peak Kaiser Wilhelmspitze after his emperor; only when Tanzania gained independence in 1961 was the highest point on the crater rim renamed Uhuru (Freedom) Peak.

Approaching Kilimanjaro across the plains of the Rift valley, the sheer bulk of the mountain and elevation of its summit snows are almost incredible. Five vertical kilometres aloft, the dazzling whiteness tops a volcanic cone the elliptical base of which measures some 80 x 40km (50 x 25 miles) – an area larger than that of Greater London. The mountain actually consists of the eroded remains of three volcanoes: Kibo (5895m; 19,340ft), Mawenzi (5149m; 16,890ft) and Shira (4006m; 13,140ft). All three were considered extinct until British mountaineer Bill Tilman discovered sulphur and fumaroles in the crater of Kibo in 1933, suggesting that it may just be dormant. The degree of erosion visible today suggests that the most recent significant volcanic activity occurred many millennia ago, and it has been speculated that Shira may, originally, have exceeded 5000m (16,500ft) in height. Mawenzi is, perhaps, the most spectacular in this respect: viewed from Stella Point (5700m; 18,701ft)

on the crater rim of Kibo, one cannot fail to be impressed by the 600m (2000ft) of jagged needles and gullies that top its west face. However, the seldom-seen eastern aspect – comprising the Great and Lesser Barranco walls – is even more dramatic with 1200m (4000ft) of near vertical rock and ice.

Glacial retreat on Kilimanjaro has, in recent years, been dramatic. The ice dome in Kibo's crater, once over 20m (65ft) high and covering an area in excess of 10km² (4 square miles), has all but disappeared. If present trends continue, it seems likely that no glaciers will remain in the foreseeable future. Whether this is due to decreasing precipitation measured over the last 150 years, or to more recent global warming, is the subject of controversy.

In July 1929, the Mountain Club of East Africa (today known as the Kilimanjaro Mountain Club) was founded in the nearby town of Moshi. Under its auspices began a programme of hut building on the mountain, which accelerated after President Nyerere inaugurated the Kilimanjaro National Park in June 1977. The park headquarters are at Marangu Gate (1800m; 5905ft), southeast of Kibo, and it is from here that the 64km (40-mile) Marangu Route (the 'tourist' route) commences.

All of the normal trekking routes on Kilimanjaro ascend *much* too fast to allow for proper altitude acclimatization and, consequently, the misery of a pounding headache mars the Kilimanjaro memories of far too many people. A prior trip up either Mount Kenya or Kilimanjaro's lesser neighbour, Mount Meru, will greatly enhance your enjoyment of the higher peak. Neither the effects of altitude nor the arctic conditions met on the summit of Kibo should be underestimated. It can be *very* cold up there! The vast majority of those ascending Kilimanjaro do so via the Marangu Route, and most do it in the

OPPOSITE INSET *A camp established at 4850m (15,900ft) – below Arrow glacier, the Western Breach and the Breach wall – experiences an afternoon snowstorm.*
OPPOSITE *With Mount Meru lying 50km (30 miles) to the southwest, a group crosses the Kibo summit plateau at an elevation of 5750m (18,860ft).*

TOP *Trekkers move through alpine heathland at 3000m (10,000ft). Trails up to this altitude pass through dense montane forest and can be extremely muddy.*
ABOVE *On top of Africa! The highest point on the Kibo-Kilimanjaro crater rim is Uhuru Peak, at a height of 5895m (19,341ft).*

THE MACHAME-MWEKA ROUTE

minimum five days (four nights) from Marangu Gate. Parties usually make for the Mandara Huts (2700m; 8800ft) on the first day, followed by Horombo Huts (3720m; 12,200ft) on the second and Kibo Huts (4700m; 15,500ft) on the third day. Then it's up to the summit and back to Kibo, and finally all the way back to Marangu Gate on the fifth day. Thus the climb is three times faster than the recommended maximum rate of ascent.

While Marangu undoubtedly offers stunning vistas of both Kili and Mawenzi from The Saddle, the huts are more like small villages and solitude will be hard to find. It is better to opt for a combination of the other routes for your ascent, and descend via the Marangu.

THE MACHAME-MWEKA ROUTE

Of the possible 'combination routes' up Kili, the 69km (43-mile) Machame-Mweka is the most diverse and requires a minimum of six days. Commencing at the end of the jeep track some 7km (4 miles) beyond Machame village (1920m; 6300ft), this relatively recent variation on the old Shira Route starts with a steep five-hour slither up a muddy jungle trail to Machame Huts (3000m; 10,000ft). In wet conditions this may feel like an exhausting epic. A gentle pace will give legs and lungs a better chance to come to terms with the rigours of such rapid ascent, and allow an appreciation of the jungle's verdant and mysterious charms. Montane forest forms a dense band between 1800m

ABOVE *From Amboseli National Park in Kenya, the summit snows of Kilimanjaro shimmer through the heat haze; on the right are the Saddle and Mawenzi.*

OPPOSITE *Looking up the impenetrable forested gorge of the Umbwe River, on the Umbwe Route; the lower part of this trail follows the crest of a spectacular ridge.*

and 2700m (5900 and 8800ft) on Kilimanjaro. Under a humid, shady canopy of enormous yellowwood and pencil cedar trees, the broad mud highway weaves its way skywards. Look out for the surreal silhouetted forms of giant tree ferns in damp hollows and gulleys. Bright balsam flowers and gladioli add vibrant splashes of colour to the impenetrable barrier of shrubbery that lines the trail. Common species are raspberries, elderberries and vernonia. Birdlife is abundant and vocal, but you will need stealth, a quick eye and great patience to actually see the retiring turacos, hornbills and parrots making all the noise.

From the Machame Huts, the recommended stages are: Shira Hut (3840m; 12,600ft), Barranco Hut (3900m; 12,800ft), Barafu Huts (4600m; 15,090ft), Mweka Hut (3100m; 10170ft) via Uhuru Peak, and finally down to Mweka village (1500m; 4920ft), ending with a drive to Moshi. This route affords wonderful panoramic views of the Western Breach and Kibo from the South Circuit Trail, covered between Wedge Shaped Buttress and Barafu. Though the stages between Shira and Barafu gain virtually no height, they are far from easy, but provide valuable time for trekkers to properly acclimatize.

Those proficient with map and compass may consider adding a day to their schedule from Shira Hut to make the seven-hour round-trip to the edge of the Shira plateau. Trails are very faint and few people venture here, but from Shira Cathedral (an exposed scramble along the summit ridge) the views are superb.

Given clear skies, this three-day traverse of the southern flanks of Kibo is delightful. Jungle gives way to timber-line forest between 2500m and 3000m (8000 and 10,000ft), with stands of African rosewood and giant St John's Wort interspersed with giant heathers and heaths (ericas). These outrageous cousins of species familiar in many other parts of the world often attain heights in excess of 10m. Drier sites are home to African sage, sugarbush (a protea species) and aromatic evergreens (helichrysums).

Above 3000m (10,000ft) the forest vanishes altogether and a sweeping band of open heath and moorland, properly called tropical alpine chaparral, extends to approximately 4000m (13,000ft). Liberally dotted across the tussocky grasslands here are magnificent other-worldly forms of giant groundsels (*Senecio* sp.), cabbage groundsels and lobelias, giving a truly bizarre character to these hillsides, especially when seen standing in silent ranks in the mist. Above the Barafu Hut, the climb to the crater rim at Stella Point is relentless and steep. Few trekkers will have the inclination to savour the plants and animals of the alpine zone as they toil upwards under the star-pierced obsidian of the African night sky.

Most will set off before midnight, having struggled to eat their supper with an altitude-suppressed appetite and managed little or no sleep. Oxygen-starved brain cells rarely think with their normal clarity, so consider the contents of your backpack carefully. Though it may be cold (-10 to -15°C; 14 to 5°F) setting off, the exertion of the climb will soon have most people sweating. Immediately upon reaching the crater rim the exposure to the elements is extreme, and great care should be taken to avoid the sudden cooling of sweat-

soaked bodies by the icy blast of the wind. The onset of hypothermia in such conditions can be frighteningly rapid and debilitating, so restrain your urge to dash to the top and pause to wrap up first.

Whatever the conditions, the hike along the crater rim to Uhuru Peak is a sensational and exhilarating skywalk. After dashing to have your photograph taken at the elaborate summit sign, take time to appreciate the wonders of Kilimanjaro. Few volcanoes can boast a crater as perfectly formed as the Reusch, and, as you head back from Uhuru Peak to begin the long descent, pause to admire the exquisitely delicate ice formations created by the ceaseless interaction of cold, humid air and the African sun, and look out for the white porphyritic crystals that weather out of the lava at the crater's rim.

UMBWE ROUTE

Experienced and acclimatized trekkers seeking something more challenging should consider the Umbwe Route. Described by Iain Allan of the Mountain Club of Kenya as one of the 'finest nontechnical mountaineering expeditions in Africa', this ascent is somewhat shorter (56km; 35 miles). It is also much more committing, and should really be undertaken by properly equipped parties with alpine experience. This involves some fairly steep and exposed scrambling higher up as opposed to trekking along well-marked trails and requires careful route-finding in poor weather, especially on the descent. The climb takes five days and makes its steep final ascent to Uhuru Peak via the Arrow glacier and Western Breach.

Commencing at Umbwe Gate (1400m; 4590ft), the first two stages are to the Forest caves (2850m; 9350ft) and Barranco Hut (3950m; 12,960ft), from where a day hike to the Great Barranco Breach wall and Heim glacier will further aid acclimatization. One could also opt to continue this way to Uhuru Peak (via Barafu Huts).

From Barranco Hut, which is more or less at the tree line, Umbwe Route heads north into the valley of the Bastions Stream before climbing very steeply up to the site of the Arrow Glacier Hut (4800m; 15,750ft), which has been destroyed by rockfall, necessitating a camp or chilly bivouac. From here the route ascends the Western Breach directly to the Great Western Notch on the crater rim. In good conditions and fine weather, this way offers an exciting scramble, with snowy sections offering those proficient with ice axe and crampons an opportunity to get off the loose and enervating screes. In anything less than perfect conditions, however, the route has major epic potential. Beyond the Notch lie the crater floor and the Furtwangler glacier, which must be crossed or circumvented before the final steep pull up to Uhuru Peak.

From Uhuru Peak one may descend any of the routes, though most trekkers will retreat the same way, having left their tent/equipment below on the way up. The descent of the western breach is especially difficult as it usually fills with cloud early in the day and route finding can be tricky.

LEFT *The constant interaction of cold, humid air and the power of the African sun creates many strange and beautiful ice formations on Kilimanjaro.*
OPPOSITE *With all of Africa at their feet, trekkers commence their descent from Uhuru Peak by heading around Kibo's crater rim towards Stella Point.*

LOCATION Northeastern Tanzania, around 500km (300 miles) from Dar es Salaam; nearest town is Moshi.

WHEN TO GO January-February and August-September.

START Machame-Mweka route: 7km (4 miles) from Machame village (southeast of Kili); Umbwe Route: Umbwe Gate.

FINISH Machame-Mweka routes: Marangu Gate.

DURATION Machame-Mweka route: min. 6 days; Umbwe Route: 5 days.

MAX. ALTITUDE Uhuru Peak (5895m; 19,341ft).

TECHNICAL CONSIDERATIONS The most serious considerations are altitude and weather.

EQUIPMENT Full high-mountain clothing is essential: gaiters, vests and leggings, down jackets, woollen balaclava, snow goggles. For the Umbwe Route add an all-purpose ice axe and crampons.

TREKKING STYLE Backpacking with porter support. Most trails are well marked and cairned. Huts other than those on the Marangu Route may be unfit for use, so camping or bivouac

equipment will be needed. Generally food is supplied by outfitters who arrange for porters to carry and cook.

PERMITS/RESTRICTIONS Ascents of Kilimanjaro must be organized through a tour company. The use of guides and porters in the national park is mandatory, but care should be taken when engaging their services. Many are superb, but some are scoundrels. Modest fees are payable for time spent within park boundaries.

DANGERS All trekkers must be familiar with the symptoms of, and necessary action for, Acute Mountain Sickness (AMS). Its dangers should not

be underestimated. Rules of thumb are: do *not* ascend once symptoms manifest, and descend if symptoms worsen at any given altitude.

MAPS *Map and Guide to Kilimanjaro*, 1:75,000 by Andrew Wielochowski. *Kilimanjaro Map and Guide*, 1:50,000 by Mark Savage.

INFORMATION

Websites: www.intotanzania.com/safari/tanzania/north/peaks/kilimanjaro/kilimanjaro-01-intro.htm

gorp.com/gorp/location/africa/tanzania/-home_kil.htm

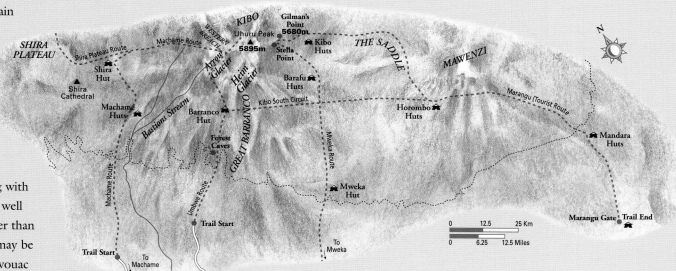

AUTHOR BIOGRAPHIES

DEAN JAMES   CHRIS TOWNSEND   DAVE WILLIS   DAVE WYNNE-JONES   STEVE RAZZETTI

Dean James has climbed and trekked extensively throughout six continents, and claimed many first ascents and first British ascents of peaks in the Himalaya, Karakorum, Pamirs, Antarctica and North America. Yet his favourite areas are the pristine wilderness and vast unexplored glaciers of the little publicized Alaska and Canadian Yukon, to which he has led 23 expeditions. On his time off, Dean writes for various British outdoor magazines. He lives in Wales.

Chris Townsend is the author of 15 books on hiking and ski touring; his latest book *Crossing Arizona*, is the story of his 1290km (800-mile) trek along the Arizona Trail. He also writes every month for *TGO* (*The Great Outdoors*) magazine. Chris has hiked the Continental Divide and Pacific Crest trails, through the mountains of Norway and Sweden, through Canada's Yukon Territory, the length of the Canadian Rockies (the first time this walk was attempted), and over all of Scotland's highest mountains. Chris lives in the Scottish Highlands.

Dave Willis is a professional adventure sports photographer and writer. He lives and works in the English Lake District, where he also runs his picture library, Mountain Sport Photography. Dave's work appears regularly in the outdoor press and in brochures in the UK and abroad and he has contributed to several books on outdoor subjects. He is also a qualified rock-climbing instructor and has led groups throughout Europe.

Dave Wynne-Jones, after an experiment in self-sufficient small-holding, turned to teaching at schools in Wales and England. He climbed for many years in Britain and the Alps before widening his horizons to include South America, Africa, Jordan, Russia, Alaska and Pakistan. His travel articles have appeared in magazines in Britain and America, and his photography contributed to the success of *The High Mountains of the Alps* (Hodders/Diadem). He lives in the Peak District near Manchester.

Steve Razzetti, trekker, guide, photographer and writer, spent his first season in the Himalaya in 1984 and has spent at least seven months of each year there ever since. Many of his exploratory routes have since become classics. He has shared trips to the Karakorum with the likes of Doug Scott, Simon Yates, Jon Tinker,

Dick Renshaw, Mark Miller and Mike Searle. Steve writes and photographs for many prestigious outdoor magazines. He authored *Trekking and Climbing in Nepal*, and was a contributor and general editor for *Top Treks of the World*, both published by New Holland.

Kate Clow was born and educated in the UK. She first pursued a career in the computer business, during which time she worked in Istanbul, selling computers while learning Turkish and studying at Istanbul University. She has since moved to Antalya at the foot of the striking Taurus range, where she has extensively explored the ancient road system on foot and motorbike. She has written a booklet on the Lycian Way, and was a contributor to *Top Treks of the World* (New Holland). Working as a writer and photographer today, Kate also leads trekking groups along ancient paths.

Seb Mankelow has climbed and trekked in the mountains of North America, East Africa, Kyrgyzstan, India, Nepal and Tibet. He has completed the frozen Zanskar River trek on three occasions. A graduate in anthropology with environmental sciences, Seb has carried out fieldwork in the Zanskar valley, and been involved in research on Zanskari irrigation and water resource management. He plans to further his academic interest in the Ladakh region with a view to spending more time with the people and mountains of South Asia.

Judy Armstrong is a New Zealander, now living in North Yorkshire, England. She is an award-winning feature writer, specializing in adventure travel and outdoor pursuits, from ski touring to mountain biking and walking. She was a contributing author to *Top Treks of the World*. Judy returns regularly to New Zealand and has travelled widely – on foot, by horse, bike, boat and bus – through North and South America, Africa, Europe and Asia.

Graham Taylor was born in Sydney, Australia. His interest in the outdoors began with camping and hiking, and his skills were further developed through canoeing, sailing and outdoor clubs. In 1986, at age 20, he completed an epic solo bicycle ride from Hong Kong to Beijing, an adventure which later led to sea-kayaking the Solomon Islands and ski-touring in Japan. In 1997, he embarked

KATE CLOW   SEB MANKELOW   JUDY ARMSTRONG   GRAHAM TAYLOR   PADDY DILLON

on a 2000km (1240-mile) solo horse trek through central Mongolia, sponsored by the Australian Geographic Society. He has since founded an adventure travel company in Ulaanbaatar, Mongolia.

Paddy Dillon, born and reared among the Pennines of northern England, is a prolific outdoor writer with over two dozen guidebooks to his name. He has walked in (and written about) every single county of Britain and his exploits in Ireland have earned him the title 'Mr Walking in Ireland'. Paddy has also walked in many parts of Europe, as well as in Nepal, Tibet and the Canadian Rockies. He leads guided walking holidays at least once a year and travels extensively. Paddy currently lives on the fringe of the English Lake District.

Ronald Turnbull grew up on Dartmoor and in the English Lake District. Based today in southern Scotland, this writer-photographer's special interest is in multiday backpack trips over rough country. He has completed 15 different coast-to-coast journeys across the UK and has written several books on the subject.Besides Picos de Europa, his European ventures include the Bernina area of the Alps. Among Ronald's dreams for the future are coast-to-coast crossings of Japan and Iceland.

Christopher Somerville is a well-known English travel writer (with some 25 books to his name), a travel journalist, and radio and TV presenter. He is the walking correspondent for the *Daily Telegraph*, and also writes extensively in *The Times* and *Sunday Times* about off-the-beaten-track travel, especially on foot, among remote communities and places in UK and Europe. He has travelled Crete from end to end and from north to south.

Sven Klinge has written a number of Australian guidebooks on walking, mountain biking and camping since his studying days at university in Sydney. His seasonal occupation as a tax accountant allows him ample time to explore the great wilderness regions of Australia and New Zealand. When not photographing the Aussie bush, Sven's interests include physics, philosophy and classical music.

Shaun Barnett is a writer and photographer based in Wellington, New Zealand. He and co-author Rob Brown won the 2000 Montana Book Award in the Environment category with *Classic Tramping in New Zealand*. In Jan 2001, together with two companions, he completed a 28-day, 248km (155-mile) tramp through the central Southern Alps, crossing 13 passes, and ascending more than 10,000 vertical metres (33,000ft).

Tom Hutton is a freelance writer and photographer with a passion for nature and the outdoors. He seeks out particularly remote or dramatic landscapes, where he indulges his love for walking, climbing, skiing and cycling. He was a contributing author to *Classic Treks* (David & Charles).

Ralph Storer was born in England but has lived in Scotland since his days at university there. After a career as an IT training consultant in industrial and educational computing, and as a lecturer at the Napier University of Edinburgh, he is today a full-time writer. Ralph is the author of a number of outdoor books, including a best-selling series of guides to the mountains of Scotland. Although he feels particularly at home in the Scottish highlands, his passion for the outdoors has expanded recently to the mountains of the American West.

RONALD TURNBULL   CHRISTOPHER SOMERVILLE   SVEN KLINGE   SHAUN BARNETT   TOM HUTTON   RALPH STORER

BIBLIOGRAPHY

NORTH AMERICA

EVOLUTION LOOP
Secor, RJ. (1999) *The High Sierra: Peaks, Passes and Trails*. Seattle WA: Mountaineers Books.
Winnett, Thomas. (2001) *Sierra South: 100 Back-country Trips in California's Sierra Nevada*. Berkeley CA: Wilderness Press.

HIGHLINE TRAIL
Adkinson, Rod. (1996) *Hiking Wyoming's Wind River Range*. Helena MT: Falcon Publishing.
Woods, Rebecca. (1994) *Walking the Winds*. Jackson WY: White Willow Publishing.

SAWTOOTH TRAVERSE
Lynne Stone. (1990) *Adventures in Idaho's Sawtooth Country*. Seattle WA: Mountaineers Books.
Margaret Fuller. (1998) *Trails of the Sawtooth and White Cloud Mountains*. Edmunds WA: Signpost Books.

ALASKA
Dufresne, Jim. (2000) *Hiking in Alaska*. Australia: Lonely Planet.
Simmerman, Nancy. (1991) *Alaska's Parklands*. Seattle: The Mountaineers.

CONTINENTAL DIVIDE
Wolf, Jim. *Guide to the Continental Divide Trail (Volumes 1–7)*. Missoula, Montana: Mountain Press Publishing.
Howard, Lynne and Leland. *The Montana/Idaho CDT Guidebook*. Englewood, Colorado: Westcliffe Publishers.
Davis, Lora. *The Wyoming CDT Guidebook*. Englewood, Colorado: Westcliffe Publishers.
Jones, Tom Lorang. *The Colorado CDT Guidebook*. Englewood, Colorado: Westcliffe Publishers.
Julyan, Bob. *The New Mexico CDT Guidebook*. Englewood, Colorado: Westcliffe Publishers.
Berger, Karen. (2001) *Hiking the Triple Crown: Appalachian Trail, Pacific Crest Trail, Continental Divide Trail*. Seattle: The Mountaineers.
Berger, Karen. (1997) *Where the Waters Divide: A 3000-Mile Trek Along America's Continental Divide*. Woodstock, Vermont: The Countryman Press.

SOUTH AMERICA

INCA TRAIL, PERU
Cumes, Carol & Lizárraga, Rómulo Valencia. (1995) *Pachamama's Children, Mother Earth and her Children of the Andes in Peru*. St Paul MN: Llewellyn Publications.
Danbury, Richard. (1999) *The Inca Trail*. London: Trailblazer Publications.

ASIA

KAÇKAR MOUNTAINS, TURKEY
Smith, Karl. *The Mountains of Turkey*. Cicerone Press.

LUKPE LA
Shipton, Eric. (1985) *The Six Mountain Travel Books*. London: Diadem. Also, Seattle (USA): The Mountaineers.
Shipton, Eric. (1938) *Blank on the Map*. London: Hodder & Stoughton.
Schomberg, RCF. (1936) *Unknown Karakoram*. London: Martin Hopkinson.
Russell, Scott. (1946) *Mountain Prospect*. London: Chatto & Windus.

ZANSKAR RIVER, INDIA
Crook, J, Osmaston, H. *Himalayan Buddhist Villages*. Delhi: Motilal Banarsidass.
Föllmi, O. (1996) *Le Fleuve Gelé*. Paris: Editions de la Martinière.

BHUTAN, HIMALAYA
Armington, Stan. *Bhutan*. Australia: Lonely Planet.
Crossette, Barbara. (1996) *So Close to Heaven, the Vanishing Buddhist Kingdoms of the Himalaya*. Vintage Books.

WESTERN MONGOLIA
Mayhew, Bradley. (2001) *Mongolia*. Australia: Lonely Planet.
Carruthers, Douglas. (1994; 1st edn 1913) *Unknown Mongolia*. London: AES.
Finch, Chris. (1996) *Mongolia's Wild Heritage*. Ulaanbaatar: WWF, UNDP Mongolia Biodiversity Project.

EUROPE

WAY OF ST JAMES
Lozano, Millán. (1999) *A Practical Guide for Pilgrims – the Road to Santiago*. Sahagún, Spain: Editorial Everest.
Raju, Alison. (1999) *The Way of St James – Le Puy to Santiago*. Milnthorp, England: Cicerone Press.
MacLaine, Shirley. *The Camino*.
Coehlo, Paulo. *The Pilgrimage*.
Raju, Alison. (2001) *The Way of St James*. England: Cicerone Press.

PICOS DE EUROPA
Walker, Robin (1989) *Walks and Climbs in the Picos de Europa*. Cicerone Press.
Roddis, Miles and others (1999) *Walking in Spain*. Australia: Lonely Planet.

PINDOS MOUNTAINS, GREECE
Dublin, Marc. (1993) *Trekking in Greece*. Australia: Lonely Planet.

CRETE
NOTE: The Greek Mountaineering Club has been preparing an English guide to E4 in Crete for several years!

AUSTRALASIA

HINCHINBROOK ISLAND
Klinge, Sven. (2000) *Classic Walks of Australia*. Sydney: New Holland (Australia).
Thomas, Tyrone. (2000) *50 Walks in North Queensland World Heritage Wet Tropics and Great Barrier Reef*. Melbourne: Hill of Content.

MT COOK/ĀORAKI
Bryant, Elise and Brabyn, Sven. (1997) *Tramping in the South Island: Arthur's Pass to Mt Cook*. Christchurch: Brabyn Publishing.
Beckett, TN. (1978) *The Mountains of Erewhon*. Wellington: Reed.
Pascoe, J. (1939) *Unclimbed New Zealand*. London: Allen & Unwin.

AFRICA

DRAKENSBERG MOUNTAINS
Sycholt, August. (2002) *A Guide to the Drakensberg*. Cape Town: Struik Publishers.
Bristow, David. (2003) *Best Walks of the Drakensberg*. Cape Town: Struik Publishers.
Olivier, Willie & Sandra. (1998) *The Guide to Hiking Trails*. Cape Town: Southern Book Publishers.

MOUNT KILIMANJARO, KENYA
Allan, Iain. (1998) *The Mountain Club of Kenya Guide to Mount Kenya and Kilimanjaro*. Nairobi: Mountain Club of Kenya.

PREVIOUS PAGES *Flanked by the Zanskar mountains and the Greater Himalaya, the Zanskar valley is generally inaccessible during summer; however, in winter much of the river freezes over, opening up an adventurous route for trekkers.*

PHOTOGRAPHIC CREDITS

KEY TO PHOTOGRAPHERS

Copyright rests with the following photographers and/or their agents.

Key to Locations: t= top; tl = top left; tc = top centre; tr = top right; b = bottom; bl = bottom left; bc = bottom centre; br = bottom right; l = left; r = right; c = centre; i = inset. *(No abbreviation is given for pages with a single image, or pages on which all photographs are by same photographer.)*

Photographers: AAPL = AA Photo Library (GM = Guy Marks)
AC = Alex Cunningham
AFP = AFP Photo (JD = Jesus Diges)
AG = Atlas Geographic (OY = Ozcan Yuksec; HO = Hakan Oge)
AH = Andrew Hallburton
AUS = Auscape (CM = Colin Monteath; FL = Ferrero-Labat; HO; LS = Lynne Stone; SW&CC = S Wilby & C Ciantar)

AVH = AL Van Hulsenbeek
AW = Art Wolfe
BBC NHU = BBC Natural History Unit (JMB = Juan Manuel Borrero; PO = Pete Oxford; TV = Tom Vezo)
BH = Blaine Harrington
BM = Bobby Model
BP = Brian Pearce
BR/SB = Black Robin Photography (SB = Shaun Barnett)
CP = Carol Polich
CT = Chris Townsend
DDP = DD Photography (RDLH = Roger de la Harpe)
DJ = Dean James
DW = Dave Willis
DWa = David Wall
DWJ = Dave Wynne-Jones
FM = Frits Meyst

GT = Graham Taylor
HA = Heather Angel
HH = Hedgehog House (CM = Colin Monteath; NG = Nick Groves)
HS = Hutchison Photo Library (FD = Fiona Dunlop)
JA = Judy Armstrong
JJ = Jack Jackson
JL = John Lloyd
JM = JS Mankelow
LT = Lochman Transparencies (BD = Brett Dennis; RS = Raoul Slater)
MH = Martin Hartley
PA = Photo Access (DR = David Rogers; PW = Patrick Wagner)
PB = Photobank (JB = Jeanetta Baker)
PD = Paddy Dillon
PH = Paul Harris
RS = Ralph Storer

RSm = Robin Smith
RT = Ronald Turnbull
SAP = South American Pictures (KM = Kimball Morrison; TM = Tony Morrison)
SC = Sylvia Cordaiy Photo Library (VG = Vangelis Delegos)
SCP = Sue Cunningham Photography (PC = Patrick Cunningham; AC = Alex Cunningham)
SK = Sven Klinge
SR = Steve Razzetti
TI = Travel Ink (JR = Jeremy Richards)
TMB = The Media Bank (DL = David Larsen; SP = Stephen Pryke)
TR = Terry Richardson
WP = World Pictures (MH = Michael Howard)

Page	Loc	Credit		Page	Loc	Credit		Page	Loc	Credit		Page	Loc	Credit		Page	Loc	Credit
Endpapers		AG/OY		48		CP		72–73		FM			br	PD		129		SK
1		HH/NG		49	bl	CT		74–79		SR		105		RS		130		SK
2–3		AG/HO			r	CP		80	t	MH		106		JL		131	t	LT/RS
4–5		CT		50		CT			b	JM		107		RT			b	SK
6–7		TI/JR		51		CT		81	t	MH		108		JL		132	t	BR/SB
8–9		MH		52–53		BH			c	JM		109		RT			b	HH/CM
12	bl	AG/HO		54	t	DW		82–83		JM		110		BBC NHU/		133	t	DWa
	br	PA/DR			b	PH		84–85		MH				JMB			c	HH/CM
13		BM		55	t	PH		86	t	JA		111		RT		134–135		BR/SB
14		BR/SB			c	DW			b	AUS/CM		112	t	SC/VD		136–137		BR/SB
15	bl	BR/SB		56–57		DW		87	t	BBC NHU/PO			b	JA		138–139		AUS/SW&CC
	br	JA		58		DW			c	AUS/CM		113	t	SC/VD		140	t	TMB/DL
16	bl	JA		59		PH		88–89		JA			c	JA			b	DDP/RDLH
	br	PA/PW		60	t	BH		90	t/b	JA		114	tc	JA		141	t	TMB/DL
17		SR			b	SCP/PC		90–91		BM			b	BP			c	TMB/SP
18		JJ		61	t	BH		92		GT		115		JA		142	l	AH
19		JJ			c	SCP/AC		93	t	AVH		116–117		JA			r	DDP/RDLH
20–21		HA		62		SCP/AC			c	GT		118		PB/JB		143		TMB/DL
22–39		RS		63	l	AAPL/GM		94–95		AVH		119	t	RT		144		TMB/DL
40		DJ			r	SAP/KM		96		AUS/LS			c	PB/JB		145		TMB/SP
41	t	BBC NHU/TV		64		DWJ		97		GT		120		WP/MH		146		AH
	c	AW		65		SAP/TM		98–99		FM		121		RT		147	t	PA/DR
42	t	DJ		66–67		BBC NHU/PO		100		PD		122		RT			c	PA/PW
	b	HA		68	t	AG/HO		101	t	HS/FD		123		AAPL		148		AUS/FL
43		DJ			b	FM			c	AFP/JD		124–125		HH/CM		149		AH
44		DJ		69	t	FM		102	tc	JL		126	t	LT/BD		150		PA/PW
45		DJ			c	FM			b	PD			b	SK		151		PA/DR
46		CP		70		FM		103		PD		127		LT/BD		154–155		MH
47		CT		71		AG/HO		104	tl	RS		128		LT/BD		160		FM

157

INDEX

Figures in bold indicate that the entries appear in photographs

Of the gladdest moments in human life, methinks, is the departure upon a distant journey into unknown lands. Shaking off with one mighty effort the fetters of Habit, the leaden weight of Routine, the cloak of many Cares, and the slavery of Home, man feels once more happy.

SIR RICHARD FRANCIS BURTON